Five Critical Things

for

Successful Book Signings

FIVE CRITICAL THINGS

FOR

SUCCESSFUL BOOK SIGNINGS

ADAM DREECE
www.ADAMDREECE.com

There's nothing more powerful than seeing a stranger transform into a fan before your very eyes.

Praise for 5 Critical Things

"Absolutely spot on. I've been doing book signings since 1990, and I thought I knew it all. Adam Dreece's clear-headed guidelines taught me a lot. You can stumble through your public appearances—or you can follow these excellent suggestions and make the most of every opportunity.

Adam Dreece has become my guru for twenty-first century publishing"
Robert J. Sawyer, Hugo Award-winning author of FlashForward

"As someone who has been stealing ideas from Adam for years, it's great to see his knowledge and experience with bookselling distilled into this succinct, clever little book. Highly recommended."
Luther M. Siler, author of The Benevolence Archives

Dedication

*To every author who has been fearful of engaging the public,
frustrated with their signings, or unsure of where to even start.*

*To my wife who makes sure I enjoy every step of this journey and
never give up.*

Contents

−1−

WHO THIS BOOK IS FOR

When I started doing book signings, and when I had my first table selling books at a comic book convention, I had no idea what I was doing. I learned a lot of lessons over the years, some much more expensive than others.

This book provides you with a map through the treacherous jungle of lessons learned, but you'll still need to take action, to walk through that jungle, in order to get to the treasures that await. Don't worry. This isn't one of those books where the author alludes to a short cut to success and leaves you puzzled as to how exactly you'd do it. I break everything down with real, actionable information.

If the idea of a book signing or having a table at a convention scares you, then this book is for you. If you aren't having the level of success you want at signings, then this book is for you. If you feel like you need to shake things up and remember what got you to where you are, then this book is for you too.

This book is NOT for people who think some magic secret will suddenly allow them to go from selling four books to four hundred at the same event without lifting a finger or challenging themselves. It's also NOT for people who sell at all costs, lying and bullying potential readers into buying their books.

To get the most out of this book, you've got to have respect for all the potential readers who offer you some of their time. The goal is not to sell to them; it's to inform and to reach them. Reaching them, in turn, leads to sales.

Note that the advice in this book does not replace writing a solid story, having it edited until it shines, and getting a cover that grabs attention. With that, and the advice in this book, you'll be ready to perform the most terrifying of duties we authors face: engaging the public.

−2−

A BIT ABOUT ME

I wasn't one of those people who always knew he was going to end up being an author. Every now and then I would secretly dream about it, and I loved taking my ideas and bringing them to life on the page, but the people I had around me for the longest time were anything but supportive. As a dyslexic, I always felt excluded when the writers I knew would go on about how you could never be a writer unless you read voraciously. I tried to focus on other things—my school, my software career, and later building my family—but I could never let writing go.

Every year or so, I'd binge-write several stories, I'd share them with a few very close friends, and then (despite their exclamations about how good my writing was) I'd bottle up the writer in me and go back to normal life. This went on for the better part of 25 years.

Then in 2009, my appendix nearly killed me. For a year and a half, I struggled with terrible abdominal scar pain and battled severe asthma as complications. Finally, I managed to get treatment to make life livable again.

I found myself at a crossroads: Either I was going to embrace my stories and ideas and do something with them, or I was going to bury that part of myself. Every story I tried to write for the next six months was contaminated with the pain of what I'd been through. As each story fell apart, I was tempted to stop . . . until I stepped back and let the pain come forward. It turned into a memoir called Refusing to Stay Down. I worked on it in secret for about six months, not even telling my wife (which was extraordinary because I normally can't keep a secret from her for more than five minutes).

Bit by bit, all the molten emotion leaked out of me unto the page of that memoir. With each step forward, I shed more of the toxic "friends" who held me back. Anyone who tried to tell me why I would clearly fail or how I would never be a real writer, had no purpose in my life. I had enough doubts and fears of my own. I didn't need people adding to them.

Then one day three years later, I found myself sitting at my kitchen table with the finished manuscript. After some serious thought, I decided I would put it on the shelf instead of release it. I wasn't going to be the guy who wrote another book about overcoming things; I was going to let that tale simply be part of my backstory.

Now freed, I could really get started. Thanks to a nudge from my nine-year-old daughter, I wrote what would become my first book: a steampunk-meets-fairy-tale adventure. Along Came a Wolf would be the seminal novel of my writing career and the foundation for The Yellow Hoods series.

At first, I didn't know what I would do with the book. I knew nothing about writing professionally, or marketing, or selling, or publishing, or a dozen other topics I thought essential. While I was toiling with indecision, my wife put me down on the waiting list for a table at a huge local comic book convention (about 95,000 attended that year).

I'd just received my polished manuscript back from my editor-friend earlier in the day when, at 10pm on March 6th, 2014, the email came from the convention organizers asking if we wanted the table.

My wife stared at me with her big blue eyes, her eyebrows raised in curiosity, her lips in a half-smile. I could hear what she was thinking. For what felt like minutes, we sat silently until she finally asked, "What do we say?"

"We say yes," I replied with a perfect blend of panic and excitement. I was going into self-publishing and would have a booth, despite having no idea how to transform the MS Word file I had into a physical book.

When the booming voice of the announcer declared the convention open and people would start streaming in, I was struck with icy terror.

Glancing at my vertical banner, my arranged books, and my table display, one thought kept running around, screaming my head: I have no clue what I'm doing. This is going to be a horrible failure. What have I done?

The first hundred people I spoke with were subjected to the absolute worst, unfocused, eye-glazing book pitches in human history. But I did one thing right starting from that day: I paid attention to people's reactions and learned from each encounter. By the end of the four-day-long event, I'd sold over one hundred books. I had no idea if that was great, bad, or okay. It didn't matter though—I was happy I'd covered more than my costs! Later I would learn that I'd done great and that I was only beginning to understand the five critical things I would need to know for consistently successful book signings.

Since then, I've written a dozen books and sold thousands of copies in person (which I refer to as hand-selling); I've sold thousands more copies online because of those book-signing appearances. In the first two years, I participated in dozens upon dozens of comic book conventions, and I appeared at over a hundred book signings. I learned a great deal then and still learn from each event I attend. I've gone from succeeding by what felt like random chance to understanding the fundamentals of what best positions an author for success.

A few years ago, I started speaking as a presenter at writer conferences. I revealed how to have a successful book signing and gave talks on the scarier elements of being an author. This led to being asked to write a book that offered more than what I could deliver in a 45-minute long speech, so here we are.

—3—

Readers Need To Discover The Greatest Things On Earth: Your Books

S ome people will argue that doing an in-person event like a book signing or renting a table or booth at a convention is a waste of time. You can't attend hundreds of them, so what's the point? Why sell dozens of books, maybe hundreds, in-person when you could focus on selling tens of thousands online? It sounds like a simple choice, but it isn't. While it's true that you can't be everywhere and that there's a limit to how many events you can do, engaging potential readers and fans is well worth it. Of the strategies that can help you build momentum, hand-selling not only works, it provides secondary benefits as well.

Interacting with readers who are excited about your work can refuel your soul, can beat back your self-doubt, and can remind you of the influence one person can have—especially when they bring a dozen friends to buy your books. I don't know any authors who don't love when a stranger becomes a fan, and live events only strengthen that author-reader connection.

Online marketing often feels like a rigged game, but meeting people doesn't. Though it can feel awkward at first, it's powerful. There's only one thing better than seeing their face light up as you tell them about your book and they clutch it tightly to their chest, and that's running into that reader somewhere unexpected, like Walmart, and them saying loudly for all to hear: "I absolutely loved your book. It touched my life." It'll happen to you if you put yourself out there.

Being present in the flesh also allows you an opportunity to gain invaluable feedback. It gives readers a chance to hear about amazing stories from the very person who came up with them and respond.

You might not feel like you are anything special, but you are. You are an author, a wielder of words and creator of universes. You weave emotion into moments and bring forth an explosion of imagination in the minds of others. We don't always feel like that, but fans can remind us that our work is not a waste of time to them.

Therefore, I can say with confidence that in-person engagement is never a waste of time for authors and leads to sales.

As a welcomed guest, authors should always treat every staff member with the utmost respect. Showing respect to the people you're working beside that day creates a positive book-signing experience for everyone.

While some staff members will come by, hear about your books, and then guide people to your table, others will ignore you. It's not personal if they ignore you; you're at their workplace. However, a gracious and grateful attitude toward staff members who do help you can lead to an on-site friend and ally.

–4–

WHAT'S A BOOK SIGNING?

A book signing is a scheduled appearance where you hand-sell and autograph print copies of your book. Often it's you at a table with your books at a book store; other times it's you at a table with your books at an organized, massive event—like a comic book convention or a book fair. However, unless you are a celebrity, you won't simply be sitting at a table signing madly as a queue of fans wait for their turns to praise your work in a few seconds before being shuttled along. Your fans get to have a real encounter with you, one that you have an opportunity to help make memorable and meaningful.

Book signings are not about sitting behind a table reading a book (by someone else, no less) or writing your next manuscript until someone asks what your books are about or if they can get a copy signed. That attitude makes an author into a bored cashier; a book signing attitude makes you both a creator and an entertainer.

Book signings are about being mentally and physically present. They're about engaging with strangers and making them fans. Engaging strangers starts with something as simple as making eye contact, waving them over, and offering a friendly, "May I tell you about my books?" This creates a no-obligation opportunity for them to discover a new favorite book and for you to share your enthusiasm for your book. If you wait for people to come to you, then you'll miss out on a lot of opportunities to grow your author fan base. Don't worry that you're imposing on them, either! You'd be surprised how many people are happy and thankful to be drawn in by an author's genuine and sincere engagement.

Authors who sit behind their tables staring at their phones (or worse!), communicate to curious customers that they are not interested in them. Authors who act like they have better things to do than be at their own book signings communicate to bookstore owners and managers that they made a grave mistake.

An author is a welcomed guest in a store or at an event. An author's presence is meant to improve either the in-store experience for their customers or the event experience for their attendees. Because the event hosts' goal is to encourage additional sales and because the event hosts have a list of other authors who want to schedule appearances, the right attitude benefits everyone. If you make your book signing appearance a positive one, then you'll net repeat book signings and event invitations. More appearances means more opportunity to expand your readership and strengthen your fan base.

As a welcomed guest, authors should always treat every staff member with the utmost respect. Showing respect to the people you're working beside that day creates a positive book-signing experience for everyone.

While some staff members will come by, hear about your books, and then guide people to your table, others will ignore you. It's not personal if they ignore you; you're at their workplace. However, a gracious and grateful attitude toward staff members who do help you can lead to an on-site friend and ally.

WHAT'S THE GOAL?

The answer is to sell books, right? The more books an author sells, then the more successful that author's signing was, right?

Not necessarily.

That type of thinking leads to sales at all costs, and one of those costs will be an author's reputation. An author's not a scam artist trying to clear out their box of Miracle Cloth and head out to the next trade show across the country. An author is a creator and a communicator. As an author, you build your brand as you build relationships

When building your author brand, the goal of a book signing is to connect with people and inform them about your books.

Sales then becomes a secondary goal which benefits from the primary goal of brand-building. That said, sales are still important. Authors want writing income. Stores want authors who sell well and who make their customers happy. Event coordinators want authors who draw attendees and who can pay for a table. While your goal is not to make sales at any cost, you're going to want to make sure you've considered and covered all of your costs as you invest in yourself and build your author brand.

By focusing on engagement, you not only take some of the pressure off yourself, you also give a different impression to people. Having exclusively a sales focus can lead to forced sales, which can boomerang back in the form of book returns, scorching reviews, or a social media storm, all of which can damage future potential sales and isn't worth it. Taking the time to properly talk to a person sometimes means you or they will realize your book is a bad fit for them. However, they might still buy it as a gift for someone else or pass word of your books on to friends.

After brand-building and turning engagement into sales comes a third goal that supports the other two: reach.

When you are a guest author doing a book signing in a store, you're most likely the only author present that day. Your aim is to connect with as many people as you can and sell signed copies of your books to them. Some aren't interested; some don't have time; some will even monopolize your attention with no intention of discussing or purchasing your book.

Instead of focusing on the rejections, focus on the people willing to stop, look, and listen. Regale them with an entertaining book pitch. Encourage them to discover an author: you. When you invest in the ones who listen instead of the some who don't, an amazing thing will happen. Word of you and your book will spread as people tell their network of friends and colleagues. We are in an era of sharing, and the encounter with you becomes social currency. This is the power of that third goal, reach; it extends the range of author branding and book sales beyond an author's book signings.

So how does reach sell books?

Let's assume one in ten people I try to engage stops to talk to me, and one in ten people who stops buys a book from me right away. That means if I approach one hundred people at my book signing, then ten people will stop to learn about my books. Of those one hundred, one will buy one of my books immediately. And of the rest of the people, some will return when I'm not around to pick up my book, which is why reach is so important.

If I reach out to a thousand people—which is less than half the number of customers who visit big box bookstores on an average Saturday—then that's one hundred people who learned about my book and ten books sold. Sometimes that number is higher, sometimes lower, but you get the picture.

My best normal book-signing day netted seventy-four sales. Additional benefits included some follow-up online sales, reviews, and people making a point to find out where I was next to get signed copies of other books of mine. The more people you engage, the greater your reach; the greater your sales.

At the heart of reach is that engaging with people can affect the now (immediate sale), affect the soon (people deciding to buy the book a few days or weeks later), and affects the future by putting in motion people talking about your books and raising interest and brand awareness. Many times I've had someone come up to me and say, "My friend was telling me about your books. I'm not normally into these types of books, but my friend says they're really good. What are they about exactly?"

At the end of the day, we want to have sold all of our books, but we acknowledge the path to getting there isn't by conning or forcing anyone. We engage the curious and we share the wonders of our stories; we respect their decision about whether or not to buy and recognize that decision will always be theirs and theirs alone. We never claim our book is something it isn't, for we know unmet expectations can result in buyer's remorse which can bite us later. We trust the power of reach, and we accept that someone choosing not to buy our books the instant we met them doesn't mean that they won't buy one or more books later (or tell someone else who will).

Now that we know what to expect at a book signing and our top three goals (building an author brand, engaging readers to invite organic book sales, and extending brand and sales reach), the next step is to prepare to turn strangers into fans at an author appearance.

How To Get A Signing

Once upon a time, I had absolutely no idea how to get a signing. I thought that maybe I had to be official in some way, though I had no idea what they might be. Maybe only publishers could set them up, and here I was, an independently published author. Maybe I needed a publicist, but I couldn't afford one.

I went around and around in my own head trying to figure it out, without actually talking to anyone who could advise me. Then, one day, my wife just walked into a local bookstore and simply asked how to have a book signing! Here's what you need to do.

First, prepare a pitch for the event coordinator, aka the book-signing scheduler. It should be quick and should explain the genre, category, and type of book to be featured at the signing. For example:

"The book is a high-action, young-adult science fiction, time-travel adventure with a strong female heroine."

or

"The book is the third volume in a tragicomic emerging-adult fantasy romance series; it's like Harry Potter mixed with When Harry met Sally."

If you have won an award or have been a finalist in a literary competition, then mention that as well. For example:

"This book was a finalist in Time Traveler Magazine's Best Fiction of the Year."

or

"I won the award for Author to Watch in the Emerging Adult Series Category from the National Fiction Guild for the first and second books in this series."

Next, be prepared to drop off a print copy of the feature book at the store for them to have a look at, and potentially, read. Bookstores have many things to consider when selecting an author for an in-person appearance, including whether the type of book fits with the customers they tend to draw in or the time of year when a book category or genre shows and sells better. If your book is a non-fiction, self-help book on how to survive Christmastime with family, but it's July and the bookstore caters to fantasy and science-fiction readers, that book would be a terrible fit.

Though it's a disappointment, not being the right fit with a particular bookstore is not a failure. If you know another author's books are the right fit for that store, then share what you learned. That author could have information to share with you about a store that wants authors who fit your book's genre, category, and type. By engaging with other authors across genres and categories, you expand your network of empathetic people-in-the-know who can keep you aware of book-signing opportunities.

The second step is telephoning and asking for the consignment manager or the events coordinator. Authors should not just show up for two reasons: Firstly, the manager or events coordinator might not have the time; secondly, just showing up puts that person on the spot for a response right then. Pressuring a manager or coordinator rarely works in an author's favor.

An author can email instead, though I find a telephone call is best. Always ask if it's a good time, always confirm who schedules author appearances, always have a message prepared for that right person, and then always be ready for that right person to have a little time to talk right then.

If the store is interested, they will likely ask you when you want to book a signing date, so know your schedule and be prepared to offer several dates for that. It's pretty typical for a book-signing coordinator to want to see an author in action and gauge sales and customer reaction before committing to shelf placement of your books.

While it's possible that an author's books are already in stock, that author should never assume the store has enough sale copies. An author should talk with the coordinator or manager to see how many books typically get sold at a book signing, for more books may be needed. If you're traditionally published, or have a distributor as a high volume independent author, this can take a while as I've learned from friends and store managers.

Because shelf space is always at a premium in stores, a manager may not (or cannot) add many (or any) copies to the store's inventory when your book signing event is done. However, a manager may choose to negotiate a consignment deal, so an author should be prepared to discuss consignment terms.

Consignment is an agreement between you and the store that essentially says you will leave books with them, for free, for x days and if they sell any, you will invoice them at the end of the month for cover price minus an agreed to discount (often 45% discount).

If your books aren't already in the store's inventory, then consignment is your friend.

One last thing to keep in mind is there is always some paperwork to do. When you drop off books, record how many copies of which titles are being dropped off. Some stores will have a consignment sheet, or you can make up your own in which case bring two copies and get yours signed (alternatively you can email them on the spot), or you can simply send an email to the store manager with the details. I've added a simple template at AdamDreece.com/5ct in case you'd like to have something handy

For events like book fairs, farmers' markets, or comic book conventions, an author should visit the event website and seek out the vendors (or exhibitors) section. After thoroughly reading the event's regulations and instructions, an author applies to reserve a paid space, or booth, at the event. Application deadlines vary, but they are usually months in advance of the event. Also, an event may require an author to turn in an application fee and a down payment on a booth rental. Even with an application fee and a down payment on rental fees, a booth may not be guaranteed.

It may seem unfair, but authors must be prepared to pay for the opportunity that organized events provide: potential readers who want to buy new books and meet new authors. Booth rental fees are connected to an event's popularity and attendance. A booth at a local event could cost fifty dollars or less; a regional or international event booth could cost hundreds of dollars, if not a few thousand.

Booth rentals at shows, markets, fairs, and conventions are investments; so are bookstore appearances. With the Five Critical Things resting on the Essential Foundation, those investments will return effective brand-building, income from book sales, and broader brand and sales reach.

–5–

The essential foundation

There's one lesson that precedes and enhances the Five Critical Things. It's not unique to book signings or even to writing, and it's quite simple: Be willing to make mistakes, learn from them, and commit to minimize their effects.

Things rarely go according to plan. Once we, as authors, accept that reality, we become ready, willing, and able to learn from every book-signing experience and can turn even the worst moments into positive ones.

Life is going to knock us off our feet and will sometimes knock the wind out of us, but we have a choice. We can wallow, or we can get up and take action. The impact of a mistake grows the longer we do nothing, and if we're committed, we can transform that panic in our belly into fuel to make decisive, immediate corrections. And once we've taken those actions, when we've got a moment to rest, then we can emotionally absorb what happened.

Those of us who do this are erroneously called lucky. Why? Because people never see the mistake happen. They never see its effects because of what we were willing to do about it. They think that everything always seems to work out for those of us who turn alarm into action.

I have made hundreds of mistakes along my way as an author. Some cost me money, some cost me time, and some shook my confidence. I learned that instead of beating myself up, instead of feeding my doubt-demons, I could focus on a forward-thinking decision I could act on; then, I did it. By the time those demons of doubt realized there was a window of opportunity to attack me, the window was closed and nailed shut. Turning pernicious anxiety into prudent action takes time to develop, but this skill has practical application for authors investing in book-signing events.

Acknowledging and accepting we will make mistakes means we can adapt to new situations, assess what's going on, and figure out a way forward.

Success as an author is a different experience, and path, for everyone. No one else has your history, personality, and skills. Therefore, a mistake that might devastate another author could lead to the most amazing moments of your career. Being open to even greater success because of a mistake is the first benefit of the Essential Foundation.

When things don't go as planned, it's natural to get frustrated. Frustration is emotional energy, often a cocktail of anger and fear. Instead of beating yourself up with "I knew it" or "I told you so", you can choose to listen to the energy's message. Fear tells us that we have an opportunity to act with courage; anger tells us that we have the energy to act right now. Let that demon of doubt that sits inside all of us go hungry and use that emotional fuel to help you focus on what to do next. Knowing the emotional energy from a mistake can be used to power taking immediate and courageous action is the second benefit of the Essential Foundation.

The third part is leaving personal baggage behind when stepping up to the public stage. This is supposed to be a fun experience, though it can still be challenging, so we want to be as focused and genuine as we can be. Sometimes we'll have more energy, sometimes less, but we want our fans to feel lifted up by talking to us, and in turn, we'll feel lifted up by them.

If something emotionally knocks us down, take a moment. Mentally dust yourself off, and get back to it. Sometimes I've rearranged how the books are set up on my table as a way to get back into the right mental place, or stepped away from my booth for a moment to call my wife for some emotional reinforcement.

We act, we strive, and we won't always succeed, but we will do a million times better than if we were just lying on the ground and submitting to defeat. When we're done, the event over, we can reflect on everything, gleaning every possible lesson and piece of insight from what happened, to make us better for next time.

Here is one of those situations that made me feel defeated. I was two-and-a-half hours into an eight-hour-long drive to a convention, with no time to spare, when I realized I'd forgotten my cash box. All the petty cash, my Square reader, everything I needed to conduct financial transactions was inside it. I pulled over on the side of the road, trying to think how I could get a new reader, replace my cash box and supplies, and go to the bank for cash when I arrived. I acknowledged the reality that everything would be closed when I arrived, and I would not be ready when the convention started early the next morning if I followed that plan.

After a deep breath, I turned the car around and chose to add the extra five hours on my drive to make sure I had everything I needed when the convention started. It turned out I'd left two important banners beside the cash box, which would have been a surprise second blow had I continued forward. I may have arrived later than I'd hoped, but everything worked out better because I chose decisively that the mistake I would live with was an added five hours to my drive.

Another time, I arrived at an event only to find that I had forgotten two boxes of books, my pricing sheets, and two banners. I stood in front of my unassembled booth, my mind racing. Then, I laughed. I laughed because the worst day in the world as an author is abundantly better than most good days in an office. I left my booth, bought a tea, came back, and came up with a new booth setup. Once again, defeat was turned into victory because I became open to greater success when I embraced that any mistake I made as an author meant I was an author and not working in an office just dreaming of being an author.

More recently, I picked up a print run of my latest book from the printer only to realize once I got home that it had the wrong price on the back. Instead of $19.99, it was priced at $12.99. I've learned that not having prices on the back can make people feel uncomfortable and can lead to reduced sales as most people don't want to ask.

Anyway, the printer was to ship books out to a store right away for me. This had come at the end of several hard months, so part of me just wanted to put my hands over my eyes and pretend it wasn't happening.

Instead, I took that fiery panic in my chest and fired off an email, telling them about the problem and to stop the shipment. I then picked up the phone and left a voicemail restating my discovery and my directives. An agonizing half-hour went by as I waited on tenterhooks for a reply.

Finally, it came in; better yet, there was a proposed solution. They could make a sticker that was nearly invisible and would cover the incorrect price with the correct one. The cost to fix that mistake was unbelievably fair.

The next day they sent me a digital proof, which looked fine on a screen. However, I didn't let out that deep breath I was holding until I was in their office examining a copy of the book bearing its correction sticker. It looked fantastic. The shipment left two days late, but everything was okay.

I learned a lot from that mistake because I put on my author persona and became strong enough to refuse defeat and to work with the printer toward a reasonable fix to our shared problem. The most important lesson I learned was that while I could negotiate a lower price somewhere else, this printing company had my back. They're as committed as I am to make my printed books the best they can be, and I will not forget it.

Fear can be a heck of a motivator if you channel it right. It can get you to take action where you may otherwise have passed up the opportunity; it can shake ideas loose that you might have otherwise automatically filtered out.

Taking a moment to harness that fear, to think, and to assess the situation is critical. On several occasions, I couldn't detach my emotions from the situation, so I called my wife. If you don't have a supportive spouse, then find a trusting friend or a fellow writer. Being able to articulate what has happened helps me figure out what I can do. This allows me to do my best to turn the situation around, or at least mitigate the damage.

If we can't allow ourselves to make a mess, to make mistakes, then we can't get out of our rut and move on to newer and greater things with the lessons we've learned and earned along the way.

With that, let's delve into the Five Critical Things.

—6—

CRITICAL THING #1:
YOU NEED AN AUTHOR PERSONA

Think of an Author Persona like a superhero mask, allowing you to do things that you might otherwise be uncomfortable doing. Every author needs one, even the people who say "I'm always me." Whether we're dealing with family or the people at work, we present ourselves differently in different contexts. We identify subjects as allowed or off-limits for those contexts. Another great example is how people act on first dates, or rather, how most people with any sense act on first dates. I was not one of those people.

Many years ago, I went on a fateful first date with a wonderful woman (who would one day become my wife) where I demonstrated my complete lack of dating skill and understanding of first-date personas. Dinner went really well, and the conversation was amazing. When we decided to go for a walk, I felt the pressure of not really knowing how dates are supposed to work when you're twenty-three years old. Why? The last time I'd gone on a first date had been when I was nineteen, and I knew things were different now.

As we sat to talk and watch the fleeting traces of the setting sun, I got more and more nervous. I went from talking like an excited river to an irrepressible tsunami. I had no idea what to say, or what I was supposed to do, so my brain decided that I needed to talk about all subjects, all at once. I was a little kid spilling my mental bucket of Lego bricks on the floor and then yelling excitedly about how there were spaceships and buildings and puppies waiting to be made. I didn't have a solid sense of who I was in general, and I had no clue how I was supposed to 'be me' in a situation like that.

By the time I realized that my date wasn't responding, it was too late. She was staring at me with a look of complete and utter disbelief, her eyebrows pulled tightly together in disapproval. She suggested that we wrap up the date, and I felt crushed. We walked back to her car, and she offered me a ride to my apartment. On the drive, I worked my way up to offer mild small talk but then to my surprise, as we pulled up to my apartment building, she asked if I'd like to hang out the next day.

I got the second date offer because she had time to process my behavior, my words, and liked me enough to risk seeing me again. Many people wouldn't have. As authors at a book signing, many of us can get as nervous as I did on that first date. This often manifests as either an avalanche of words on poor unsuspecting passersby, or as standing there silently as they walk by and we argue in our heads about what we should say. The key problem is not having defined who we are in moments like that, and that's exactly why we develop our Author Personas.

When we assemble our Author Personas, we need to identify the elements of ourselves we're going to include—some of which we will turn the volume up on, and others we'll turn down. An Author Persona is our public-facing, refined—yet still genuine—version of ourselves. I like to think of my Author Persona as the baggage-free, cleaned up, more optimistic version of who I usually am otherwise. It's the best me I can envision, not a copy of someone else.

The Author Persona is also like a suit of armor for two key reasons: restraint and resolve.

Firstly, the mental armor allows us space from things that would otherwise make us react. We will need to be even-tempered and reasonable. If someone says something offensive, I react differently. In my Author Persona, I'm much more conscious of context. I'm a public figure, so my words and actions could show up on YouTube and be brand damaging.

Secondly, the mental armor allows us to do things that we would never otherwise do. We need to be assertive and courageous. For me, that includes attending social events where I don't know anyone and chatting with people. Normally, I would rather hide in the corner, or better yet, flee. Wearing my Author Persona, I adopt a different view on of the people in the room and the purpose of the event, so I will walk up to strangers and greet them. I'll admit it's weird, particularly as this starts becoming second nature, but I'm so glad I have it. I've met some amazing people that I would have never approached.

The best place to start thinking about your Author Persona is working backwards from a best-case encounter at a book signing. Imagine a potential reader walking up to you. Fast-forward through them interacting with your Author Persona for a moment. Now they're leaving, hugging your book, a glowing smile, a newly minted fan. How did that happen? Who was the genuine Author Persona that they met? For me, I imagined them having met someone who was down-to-earth, funny, and who was excited about his stories.

With our ideal public author selves firmly in mind, each of us can gather our personal strength and our strengths as a person and can develop an Author Persona.

HOW I DEVELOPED MY AUTHOR PERSONA

Once upon a time, the very idea of standing behind a table talking to random strangers about stories I'd somehow written and self-published would have made me laugh hysterically. Talking to rooms full of people about writing stories? Yeah, right. My biggest challenge was I couldn't see myself as being able to do that.

If you met me today at a book signing or conference, you might find this hard to believe. It all seems so natural now. Someone else in my place might offer a grin and say, "All it took was hard work and practice. You can do it too!" but I'm not that type of guy.

It took time and recognizing that I had already gathered the basic skills I needed over my career so far, but it wasn't enough. I needed a way to bring my down-to-earth and funny author side out, without hesitation, when talking to strangers about my stories, which felt extremely personal. That was the start of my Author Persona.

When I was a teenager, I played enough Dungeons and Dragons to have earned a Ph.D. in storytelling. By age 15, I realized that I could give traits to my characters that I could bring into my real self after enough practice. Role-playing was like a laboratory where I could incubate traits and skills, try them out, and if they felt right, I would try them out in the real world.

The weirdest thing happened.

Pretending to have leadership skills translated into actual leadership skills. It was exhilarating the first time someone referred to me as a natural leader. I'd never thought of myself that way.

Flash-forward to a snowy day in Calgary, Alberta, Canada, circa 2013. I had been working on an autobiographical manuscript for three years that I would soon toss aside. The first book I would be known for—a steampunk fantasy adventure that would launch both a young-adult series and my writing career—and my first comic book convention to promote it were a year away. With no idea either was coming, I was unaware how much my life was about to change.

I was standing in a coffee shop, taking a break from my stressful full-time job and wondering if I should even bother continuing to write. I was thinking through what successful authors needed to do and know, and I was worrying about public speaking. The idea of meeting people and putting myself out there was terrifying. Then one of my software developers walked in.

"Hey, Boss."

For some reason, his words jarred me from my thoughts. The memory of first daring to try my fledgling leadership skills as a teen came to mind. As the developer got his coffee and left, I wondered if I could do with public engagement skills what I had done with leadership skills. I'd done the same thing with my ability to give speeches to large groups a few years before.

I decided I could, but how?

First, I listened to a bunch of audiobooks and podcasts. They were useless, preaching all the same old, same old: Self-proclaimed experts tell you what to do, but always stop short of the useful and necessary explanation of how to do it. Though discouraged, I was still determined.

Then I happened upon *The Charisma Myth: How Anyone Can Master the Art and Science of Personal Magnetism* by Olivia Fox Cabane. I read it, and then I listened to the audiobook. It made sense to me, so I learned what I needed to try out my fledgling public engagement skills.

Summoning up the amount of courage that one might imagine is required to take on a dragon with a spoon, I walked into that familiar coffee shop. With a quick glance at the barista's name tag, I took my first step on the road to speaking in public like a successful author.

"Hey, Shelley. How's your day going?" I said. I sounded like I was asking my mom.

Shelley stopped, the glassy look in her eyes quickly replaced with the sudden realization that I was engaging with her as a person instead of playing out the conventional drink-ordering process. She frowned, thrown off, replied quickly, and moved me along.

When I picked up my tea, I thanked her by name. My hands were shaking when I left.

I said hi to Shelley and her co-worker the next time I came in. By the fifth time I did it, both greeted me as I walked in. Once I had built that casual connection, I asked if I could get their thoughts on the summary of a book I had in mind. For the first time, I offered my clumsy, awkward pitch to my new acquaintances.

Encouraged to refine that skill, I tried speaking to people when we first entered an elevator. I decided to say nothing intellectually profound, just something that would fit the moment and make the person look up from the floor or away from the screen mounted above the doors. I was pleasantly surprised that I connected with most of them.

Practicing casual conversation taught me to connect quickly with people and also how to handle the rejection that is part of dealing with the public, especially when you're behind a table. I learned it wasn't personal when they shift their gaze elsewhere or pretended they didn't hear me. Instead of focusing on those people, I learned to focus on the ones who graced me with a moment of their time, who allowed us to have a moment.

All of this experience gave me the confidence to keep going. I felt that the author I wanted people to one day encounter starting to develop within me. I was developing the best me—as a successful author and a genuine person—I could envision.

Months later, when the doors opened at that fateful comic book convention where I launched my first book, I was still terrified, but it didn't feel completely alien. I had my initial book pitch and my fledgling Author Persona. Every time I spoke to someone about Along Came a Wolf, both pitch and persona improved.

Over the next two years, I met thousands of people and had thousands of conversations. I learned which subjects added to the experience of meeting an author in person, which ones were selfish and served no purpose, and which ones were potentially damaging to me as an author and a public speaker. For example, talking about writing or about being a dad is great. Complaining is not. Arguing politics or criticizing a particular thing or person is dangerous. I learned that if authors always assume someone's recording what we're saying, because they very well might be, then we're in the right frame of mind to make meeting us in person a great experience for our loyal readers and our potential readers.

As time went on, I came to realize the most important part of developing my Author Persona was learning who I was as an author. I asked myself some hard questions: What stories am I telling? What stories do I want and need to tell? What do I stand for? What type of stories won't I write?

I never thought much about who I was as an author until my good friend, fellow author and awesome podcast host, Josh Pantalleresco of Just Joshing, pointed out that too many authors he interviews don't know who they are. They've built 90% of their Author Persona, but they forgot the most important ten percent: Who they are for the public. All too often authors come across as just a person who wrote some stuff. They didn't know what elements of themselves they put into their writing, nor how they wanted to be remembered by people.

As our Author Persona develops and evolves, it builds our author brand and is tied to it.

BRAND YOU

An author's brand is made up of the Author Persona that people encounter, the author's social media posts and other online activity, and the contents of the author's published books. Together, it communicates a set of values and messages that people come to expect and to trust. If we, as authors, do anything that's radically outside of this set of values and messages, our readers can feel betrayed—or at least confused. More than once I've seen a children's author act inappropriately in public or online. Making really crude jokes on Twitter with an author account may burnish the author brand of a noir detective stories, but it could badly damage the brand of a children's author.

That might sound unfair. Why should our personal politics and opinions be limited by an author's brand? Well, it's about setting and building up expectations.

Let's use a theoretical example to understand brand through a fictional footwear manufacturer: Great Feel.

I like Great Feel shoes. I've owned their sneakers and have liked them for years. I recommend Great Feel when people are looking for new sneakers. If I were hunting for some winter boots and saw Great Feel were now selling boots, then I would trust that those boots were well-made and would strongly consider buying a pair of them. A shoe manufacturer making boots is reasonable, right?

What if Great Feel were suddenly selling burgers instead of boots? I would have a confused, record-scratch moment. Burgers wouldn't fit with the shoe brand that I know and trust. I wouldn't be able to keep from imagining myself eating sneakers if I bought one of their burgers. It doesn't mean that Great Feel couldn't ultimately convince me their hamburgers were good; it's just that it would take time and effort to do so. There's an amount of shock that I'd need to get over before I trusted a shoe manufacturer could also be a food vendor.

It's all about expectations, boundaries, and understanding the consequences of what you bring into the scope of your brand. With family, you might avoid social politics for the sake of family peace; as an author, voicing your political views and social philosophy might be a core part of your Author Persona, or not. Determining whether you are ready for the consequences to publicly engage on hot-button issues is important.

I got to watch from the sidelines a few years ago when a well-known fantasy author I followed kicked off a debate about Middle East politics out of the blue one day, throwing his opinion around like a wrecking ball. Within an hour, social media swallowed him. There were people on all sides, plus trolls and bots. Every tweet he put out afterward, regardless of content, would be pounced upon and the political debate and fury continued. It took nearly a year before social media calmed down. The author, however, wasn't the same afterwards.

Having a clear sense of our author brand doesn't mean we can't advocate for our deeply held beliefs. It means we need to be conscious of what, and how, we incorporate them.

Personally, and as an author, I am a strong believer and supporter of LGBTQ+ and women's rights. My stories reflect this deeply held belief, even though I never plant political flags or derail the story to make a statement. I decided that I could live with the consequences of integrating these beliefs into my books, into my author brand, and into my Author Persona. I have lost sales, as well as speaking engagements, due to these beliefs and I am fine with that. Losing those are more acceptable to me than hiding my position on two social issues that I see as fundamentally important for our time. And for the record, I believe I've gained far more than I lost when it comes to sales and opportunity. The critical thing is that I don't believe I could be genuine in my Author Persona without these beliefs playing a part.

Individually we need to figure out what issues align with our brand, and which ones don't. This does not mean that we never talk about the things which do not align, it means that we are very conscious of where and when.

How an author acts in public, online, and through the written word all comes together in this strange amorphous thing called brand. Being out in public and meeting people directly impacts author brand, and that means a developed Author Persona, even a fledgling one, is necessary to protect that author brand.

Your author persona is who you are in the public arena, and brand is about what people are expecting based on your past books and activities. The brand is bigger than you, it's the business cloud that surrounds you. Trust in your brand often tips the scales when people are considering taking the risk to try your latest book or recommending it to someone.

DEVELOPING YOUR OWN AUTHOR PERSONA

A strong Author Persona originates from being deliberate with what personality elements you include, deciding what you want to communicate, and knowing what you consider off-limits. There have been times when I had to end conversations with potential readers because I saw no good could come of it.

Even if you've done a lot of book signings already, there is a huge advantage to organizing your thoughts into author-specific edition of you for engaging the public. An Author Persona is useful beyond book signings, conventions, and conferences. We get invited to give talks about being a writer at schools, functions, and author panels as well. We also get recognized when we don't expect it. More than once I've been with my kids at Costco or Walmart (and once at a "Weird Al" Yankovic concert), and someone came up to me asking if I was Adam Dreece. Immediately, I slipped into the comfortable suit of my Author Persona, rather than being in dad-mode. Whatever is in my mind when I put on that Author Persona, whatever burdens are on my shoulders, them get automatically put aside. I'm then able to engage a fan or a potential reader as I'd like to.

Step One: What's in a Name?

I have a snarky one-liner I like to use when talking about the value of a good name: "A rose by any other name would cost half as much." Names are powerful, so expectations come along with them. When I thought about being in front of people as an author one day, it was paralyzing to imagine my real name linked to my writing career and any potential failure as an author for the rest of my life. I had a career in software and felt some people I regularly encountered would look unfavorably on me for writing books for young adults. Add to that the doubt demons who jumped up and down on my shoulders, reminding me of all the negative feedback that had been thrown at me in my early years by "proper" writers, and I was rooted to the spot, unable to move forward at all.

I wished I had a mask I could put on, like a superhero. Among other things, it would allow me to be more genuinely me than I ever allowed myself to be. I needed something to help turn my paralyzed dreams into high-velocity reality, little did I realize that a name can do that.

As I brought my autobiography to a close, this notion of needing a fresh start was eating at me more and more. I stood back from my true story about conquering bullying, dyslexia, horrible scar pain, medical mishaps, and more, and realized I didn't want to be that guy. The guy connected to that book was damaged, not triumphant. The manuscript was burdened by emotional and psychological baggage, and it almost felt like I'd written an apology about not being good enough to be a real writer. Instead of trying to rewrite it to make it work, I scrapped it. The manuscript's real value had been to drain the pain out of me. Now I could really get started on being an author.

I started writing the initial draft of Along Came a Wolf, knowing it was time to fulfill my dream and become a published author. Thoughts about that superhero mask—a fresh identity and spotless reputation to make that future happen—came back to mind. That's when the name of my Author Persona came to me: Adam Dreece.

As Adam Dreece, I could be who I wanted. The name was my mask, or more accurately, it was the secret that let me remove the everyday mask I wore and be my true, creative, daring self. I could set aside my personal-life baggage. I could release the fear that any mistake I made as an author would ruin the name and reputation I'd made in technology. That pen name, Adam Dreece, had the potential to become the best me I could envision.

I had found my superhero mask, and it fit perfectly.

Even if you've published seventy books under the name Anne Smythe, you can still decide that, going forward, your Author Persona is Annie Smythe. Annie could be that sharp-witted, kind-hearted, dark sense of humor side of you. Annie could be friendly yet won't talk about her personal life or politics, ever. Annie smoothly turns the focus of those conversations back to her books and her fans and her potential readers, or Annie politely brings those chats to a close.

Our names possess value and power. Even if we don't often think about it, expectations come with our names and our current lives, which means we must ask ourselves: What in my life would need to change for me to become a successful author?

It could be just a tiny tweak of how we present ourselves. It could be no more than choosing a nickname or our initials. However, it also could be a pen name that makes us hold our heads higher, move our shoulders back further, and smile while making eye contact longer. Whatever we decide, the naming of our Author Persona must be an intentional decision.

Step One is all about deciding on what mask you need, and what the world should call you.

Step Two: Are We All Imposters?

In a Tumblr post on his official page, Neil Gaiman shared a personal story about impostor syndrome. He was attending an event lasting several days that celebrated luminaries in the arts and sciences.

As he stood the back of a hall, he started speaking with an older gentleman. They talked about many things, including that they shared the same name: Neil. The older Neil then revealed to Neil Gaiman that he didn't feel he belonged at the event. Surrounded by creators and inventors, he felt like an impostor because he went where others had sent him.

The older Neil was Neil Armstrong, the first man to walk on the moon.

At the heart of this anecdote is the idea that anyone can be troubled by doubt. We can doubt our abilities, our skills, our right to be where our hard work has brought us. However, doubt doesn't have to stop us from moving forward with our dreams. In fact, doubt can keep us grounded, sharp, and appreciative of what we receive.

I was at a book store setting up for a book signing appearance, when an excited squeal got my attention. As I turned to see what the commotion was about, I saw a teenage girl grab her father's arm and say, pointing right at me, "That's him! That's my favorite author. The one I was telling you about. I read four of his books, and look, he's got a new one!" Someone who was a fraud couldn't have created a genuine moment like that; I earned such a wonderful fan and appreciated that she was as excited about reading my stories as I was about writing them.

So how do we advance from potentially crippling doubt to earning and appreciating those types of moments? We need to start by fixing our mindset.

A Helpful Exercise

It's not sufficient to just read this exercise and nod and say to ourselves, "Yes, I get it."

Actually do it.

First, we find a quiet place with a mirror where no one will hear or interrupt us. The mirror needs to be large enough to see our whole face. Then, staring into our own eyes, say three times slowly, "I am a purple, bubble-headed unicorn."

Many of us likely will be frowning. We may even be wondering what the heck the point is of saying something so silly, but trust me. If we can't look in the mirror and say that without moving our eyes, then we try again the next day. We repeat this exercise every day until we can speak those words three times without shifting our gaze from our own reflected eyes.

Next, we forge ahead from the ridiculous to the ego-bruising. It's the same exercise, but we are going to say, "I am a genius." The goal, this time, is to say it slowly three times without throwing up any mental shields or emotional defenses. We need to be able to say anything to ourselves, so this requires steady patience and resolute honesty.

This exercise, which I learned many years ago, took me nearly nine months to perform successfully. I was shocked I couldn't do it the first time I tried. Calling myself a genius should have boosted, not bruised, my ego! Even though I was complimenting myself, something inside me wouldn't let me accept it. This went on day after day, month after month, until finally one day, something changed in me.

Once we can call ourselves a genius for three days in a row without any defensiveness or loss of eye contact with our reflections, we move on to the last part of this mental exercise. With that same mirror, and without raising our defenses or looking away from our own eyes, we speak three times slowly: "I am an author. I am a writer. I write stories people want to read."

This is tough for a lot of people, and it may take a while to do. If we can't convince ourselves that we are real authors and not impostors, no one else is going to buy it.

Step Two is about convincing ourselves that we have earned the right to be successful authors and we aren't conning anybody. We are not imposters.

Step Three: What Are Your Values and Your Brand?

Now that we've lain the foundation of our Author Personas, it's time to raise the frame of personal values to build your public-facing Author Persona around.

What characteristics or traits do successful authors express and possess? From the catalog of all that is genuinely you in everyday life, what skills and talents and personality traits support your vision of yourself as a successful author? What core values or ideals of yours do you want to nurture and spotlight? Which core values and ideals are so much a part of your genuine self that they cannot be suppressed?

For me, I started with:

• Be down to earth.

• Try to always be positive.

• Be willing to inspire people by being open about my dyslexia, chronic pain, and severe asthma.

• Accept my books aren't for everyone.

• Be the mentor I wish I'd had.

• Share what I know with others; don't hoard knowledge.

Take a few minutes and write down a handful of ideas for yourself along these lines. Then keep that list on you. Look at it daily over the next week. Tune it whenever inspired to do so. Remove items that don't hit the mark; add new ones. Ultimately, you want to pare this down to as few points as possible. More than ten isn't helpful; five or six is ideal.

It's also good to list positive characteristics that make you uncomfortable. You will build confidence and evolve as an author and a person by pushing yourself to practice and strengthen those attributes. As I learned by playing Dungeons and Dragons years ago, practiced traits can become second nature.

Step Four: Ready for a Test Run?

Being in the public eye (no matter how small our spotlight) will challenge us. The over-thinkers like me will want to figure everything out before we try, and that's a mistake. You need to try, learn, improve, try, learn, improve, repeat. With just a very rough idea of where we're going, we can get started.

Experience is invaluable. It may feel weird at first, but that's because we're trying something different. Taking action will lead to new ideas and can lead to discovering covering the right answer, which may not have been available to us if we'd just sat in our bedroom, under the blankets, obsessing and over-analyzing. You may not have known that your smile could draw people from across a room, until someone tells you, "I have to say, I had to find out what you were smiling about."

Your Author Persona will evolve as you use it, so the sooner you try it out, the sooner you'll be comfortable with it. It will become a second skin that you don't even think about. It's like Bruce Wayne seeing trouble, pushing his shoulders back, drawing himself up to his full height, his eyes narrowing as he assesses the situation. Even before he's in the suit, he's Batman. He's always really Batman. You're always the author, you just won't be showing it all the time.

SUMMING IT UP

We all use different aspects of ourselves between work, close friends, and family. As published writers, we also need to develop a version of ourselves that we use while engaging the public: an Author Persona. It can be our armor when we're nervous and can act like a super-hero's mask when we want our true courage to shine through. The most important part, however, is that our Author Persona always remains genuine for our fans, our potential readers, and our author brand.

—7—

CRITICAL THING #2:
THE RIGHT MINDSET IS KEY

This idea needs to be the cement for your courage and your North Star for a positive mindset: There is no one in the world that a potential reader would rather hear about a book from than the author themselves. They don't want to hear from your publicist, your friend, your editor, or anyone else. No one else created the story. You did.

Some authors have insisted to me that they are so terrible—so abysmal!—at pitching their own books that they think they would harm more than help their sales. They view author appearances from only their perspective, and that is through a lens coated in fear and doubt.

To potential readers (even more so for fans), meeting an author is a magical experience. We created a realm from thought and bottled it. We provided the means for that person to join us there, an enchantment in black and white—be it a print book or an electronic publication. No matter the story we wrote, an author appearance is equivalent to having an authenticated photo of Bigfoot having tea at their house: Everything about us and how we talk to them will become part of a broader story. No matter how awkward we feel the encounter will be, fans want us. They don't want to meet people who represent us. Imagine the difference between meeting your favorite actor and meeting their event handler? Which one would you stand in line to meet?

The act of meeting us is social currency. It has value on its own as an anecdote that can be shared. Not appearing at our own book signing is also an anecdote which can be shared, and which will inevitably cause that harm we're worried about. That is all the more reason to get better at engaging people.

THE DIRTY WORD

For some of us, the words sales and selling get under our skin. It can make us feel like we're supposed to impose our wills on others. The idea of it feels wrong, even though we know selling is normal and being at a book signing is largely to sell books. The thing is, imposing our will, forcing people to buy things, that's not selling. That's bullying or swindling people. There's no integrity there.

What we need to do is provide people with an enthusiastic presentation about our books, answer their questions, and lastly make it clear that our books are available for purchase. Some authors almost hide the fact that their books are for sale; it's nothing to be ashamed of or feel uncomfortable about. We aren't offering cheap or stolen wares. We have treasure! Treasure available for the curious and intrigued.

We all dream of having those events where we sell out of our books. So, how do we do that?

First, we lift the pressure off ourselves to sell all of our inventory. Some days will be great sales days, and some won't—no matter what we do. If the weather suddenly became sunny and warm after days of gloom and rain, then I'm sorry, but the people, they ain't coming. There are all manner of situations that can arise which will limit the number of people who come to the venue we are at. All we can do is try to make the best out of the situation we're presented with.

Second, we find a way around any mental block about selling. We aren't going to use tricks or intimidation to compel customers to buy from us. We are going to use our enthusiasm and our passion to excite them. We use our experience and knowledge to inform them, and we shepherd them through not knowing who we are and what our books are about up to the point where they have a financial decision to make. The funny thing is, that last part can be tricky. Many of us can get over doing the first two things, but the last one? I had to realize that I had a subtle mental block here long ago.

I learned just how hard all of this was for me back in 2014, at that very first comic convention, when the very first person was walking in the direction of my very first book signing booth. Everyone I knew thought I would do amazingly well out of the gate, but I felt like I was wearing concrete boots for a marathon.

It took a few tries, but I got over my anxiety at interrupting strangers as they walked by. They didn't seem to mind me asking them if I could tell them about my books. I was entertaining people and starting to have fun, but I wasn't selling yet. I wondered if it would happen later, or maybe I hadn't found the right type of people willing to take a chance on a new author.

After talking to dozens more and seeing several of them get excited but still leave without my book, I figured the problem might be with me. I paid attention to my words and actions over my next encounters and realized something: I never said or did anything to make it clear my books were for sale. Was that a problem? I mean, the pricing sheet was right there. Why else did I have a booth? Surely people were seeing that, weren't they?

I stepped away from my booth and looked up and down the long row of booths I was in. There was an overwhelming amount of visual stimuli. There were t-shirt and toy vendors and artists of all sorts. Was I being lost in all of it? Maybe people were expecting vendors to be a bit more direct about selling, given the type of event.

With a heavy sigh and a grumble, I decided to kick myself out of my comfort zone. As it turned out, the next person who came by made it clear that I shouldn't take anything for granted and needed that kick.

I started with my standard soft-opener: "May I tell you about my book?"

The middle-aged, bearded man stopped and stared at me, confused.

"May I tell you about my book?" I repeated, motioning at a pile of my books.

He backed up and took in my display. "You're an author?" he asked.

"I am."

"And is this your book?"

I smiled, unable to believe I was being asked the question for the hundredth time that event. "It is. If you have a minute, I'd like to tell you about the story."

The man drew in a breath and came up to the edge of the table. "By all means," he said folding his arms and pulling on the edge of his beard.

After I finished my clumsy pitch, he picked up the book and looked it over.

I'd been at this point many times before. With my gut doing somersaults, I decided not to just stand there quietly this time. "I have them here on sale for $10 today. Signed, of course." Getting those words out was painful for me.

"Oh, you're selling them?" He looked about; his eyebrows arched in surprise. "I didn't realize people sold books at these events."

Bingo.

He flipped through the book, read a few random passages, and then nodded decisively. "I'll take one."

I couldn't believe it. I still remember his name to this day: Bob. For the next two years, Bob sought out my booth at the annual comic book convention. He always picked up the latest book for himself plus copies for his niece and for other family members.

There was nothing magical about what I said to Bob, or the other hundred and seven passersby that bought my book that first year at the convention. Those sales happened as part of talking to thousands of people. Thousands. My throat was sore, but I kept on talking. Each time, I improved my pitch, learned how different people react to different pitches, and discovered what I should not be taking for granted.

As I did more events, I came to realize that people are often in their own little worlds when I first reach out to draw them in. What's more, many don't necessarily realize that my books are for sale unless explicitly told so. Some aren't familiar with authors doing signings, while others don't necessarily expect books to be sold at the event, like Bob.

Two years later, my sales at that same convention were more than four times what it had been that first year. I had readers coming back again and again for the latest books.

As I started giving talks and helping other authors improve, I realized a few key things about selling without *selling*:

- We are offering an opportunity to entertain and inform readers about books they likely aren't aware exist;

- We are providing an occasion for readers to ask burning questions about books that only the author can answer;

- We are giving readers a rare chance to get a signed or personalized copy of a book or several books.

- We must accept that our books have actual financial value. We are not selling broken car parts as new. We are providing pieces of our heart and soul, woven into an entertaining escape, done to the best of our ability. They are worth more than 2 lattes.

To be fair, not everyone is bothered by the idea of selling. Some people get excited about it, and to them I say: don't get caught up in selling over doing right by your potential fans and your brand. Every event is an opportunity to add to your fan base. That means integrity and creating a memorable experience is key.

The last part of dealing with the issue of sales is what to do with the awkward silence that can arise as someone mulls over your book. You drew them in, you gave them the pitch, they picked up the book and started looking at it, and now it's like something's gone off the rails. Neither of you seem to know what to do. It's like social standoff of introverts. Someone needs to do or say something, and that someone is you. For these moments, I have a few strategies to suggest:

- Do you have any other questions? —Information
- I'd be happy to sign a copy for you. —Service
- I must warn you, the books do bite. —Comedy

These usually illicit a response, my favorite being a laugh from comedy ones but sometimes comedy falls flat. It's rare that a situation where I need to explicitly ask someone if they are interested in buying the book or not, but it does arise.

We each find our way to sell, but the heart of this is to make it as genuinely you as possible, and a positive experience for the reader. The worst two things I've seen an author do is thrusting a book into someone's hands saying "It's ten dollars. I take cash or credit" and the other is plucking the book from someone's hand saying, "I guess you're not really interested."

The act of "selling" can be thought of as simply sharing some information and passion about your stories, and being of service to the stranger as they make up their mind. Engage, inform, and support. That's how we'd like to make our minds up, isn't it?

BROADCASTING AND THE POWER OF THE POSITIVE

Have you ever looked at someone and been unable to stop yourself from smiling? What about finding your mood evaporate because of someone's stormy one?

When we're at our book signing table, our mindset can draw people in or repel them. Whatever we're thinking or however we're feeling will be on our faces and broadcast for everyone to see. This is awesome when things are going well. We're engaging with lots of people and selling books hand over fist. It's awful, however, when we're in a rut or a lull.

It's very important to detect when we're slipping into a negative state of mind. Are our arms folded? Is our head bowed? Are we unintentionally glaring at people? Are we intentionally glaring at people? That's not going to win people over. We've got to pull ourselves out of it if we sense that our actions appear hostile or defensive.

It's so important to have a thought that can bring us back, an emergency happy thought as it were. (Stay with me, skeptics!) This one positive thought is our rope to climb out of the pit we're in. It's a precious lifeline when we're in dire straits.

I have a built myself a bank of happy thoughts, as sometimes just one isn't strong enough to mentally reset me.

One is of my daughter's proud face when I came and spoke to her school. I was there all day, talking to one class after another, from grade five to nine. She was beaming for weeks.

Another is of a fan in a homemade yellow hooded cloak, holding the first of my Yellow Hoods books. She was so excited she could barely ask for the second book.

A third one is of my youngest son, at age five, when he was asked what he wanted to be when he grew up. He answered: "An author, like my dad."

Many times, I've been somewhere and caught myself with my arms folded or wondering if I was wasting my time. That's when I pull one of these thoughts forward and start thinking of the privilege I have of being there as an author.

Next, I remind myself that of the thousands of people who talk about writing a book, I did it. Of the thousands of people who wrote books, I'm putting myself out there, meeting people, inspiring other writers, and doing an actual signing. On top of all that, I know a lot of people who have told me they love my work. If that won't pull me out of the doldrums, I eat a snack to boost my mental and physical energy, or I take a walk and grab a cup of tea to shake things up. There are few things like smelling the aroma of the tea and feeling it warm my hands and soul.

As authors, we are amazingly immune to people complimenting our works and incredibly vulnerable to the smallest disagreeable remark (never mind damning criticism!). My cache of positive thoughts leads me to remember a happy reader, which in turn makes my shoulders relax. Without thinking, I draw in a deep, calming breath. Before I know it, potential readers are approaching with smiles on their faces, clearly interested in my display.

There's nothing like consciously changing our state of mind and then having someone come over and say, "I saw your posters and noticed you had this absolutely joyous smile. What are your books about?"

BOOM! We're back in the game. It happens to me regularly; by banking our happy thoughts and practicing our attitude-boosting strategies, it can happen regularly to all of us.

Another place where this is really important is remembering that we are a community, we authors. We aren't competitors. Yes, people have limited money—but it's not like people are shopping for a stove. They need one stove; that's it. Books? How many of us secretly wish that we could live in a building of books with a small bed and a bright reading light?

Before I published *Along Came a Wolf,* I'd never felt like part of a community. I was always a loner, never fitting in, and then a stranger showed me that I was part of my local writing community.

I was doing a book-signing appearance at a big box store when a friendly stranger came up to me. She started talking to me like she knew me, and I definitely didn't know her. She didn't ask about my books; instead, she asked if she could buy me a tea from the coffeeshop. I wasn't sure how to react, but eventually I said yes.

When the lady returned, she shared that she was an author, as well, and had done her own signing at the same store, in the same spot, the weekend before. She complimented my display, listened to my pitch, said she really liked both, and then welcomed me to the community of local authors. Aviva Bel'Harold has since become a good friend.

Her intervention filled me with positivity, and I went on to have an outstanding sales day, despite it being a quiet day in the store. The manager laughed with me at the end of the day, asking if I'd sold copies of my book to EVERY person to have come through the store.

Believe it or not, our mood affects those around us. It can draw people in as well as repel people. Keep that in mind.

SUMMING IT UP

If we go into something expecting to fail and behave like it doesn't matter, then there's a high likelihood we're going to fail. If we go into something expecting to triumph that's not much better. As soon as the numbers start to look less than what we'd planned, our moods could darken and we'll sink ourselves. It's best to go in with a strong positive mindset, appreciative that we get to be an author and determined to do our best. We push ourselves to engage more people, and if the sales are there, great. It's about reach first and foremost. The more people we reach, the better we'll do over time.

When we find ourselves in a negative state of mind, we need at least one happy thought to salvage the day. Close our eyes, focus on those good thoughts, feel the corners of our lips turn up, and we're back in the game. That happiness will help draw in potential readers and spread outward as author brand-building, sales, and reach.

—8—

CRITICAL THING #3:
KNOW THE TYPES OF PEOPLE YOU'LL MEET

U p to this point, we've talked about how we present ourselves to the public, between our Author Persona and our healthy mindset. Now let's turn the tables and focus on the people who are going to be passing by our table: our potential readers. The better we understand them, their needs, and their mindsets, the better prepared we will be to engage them.

I had no idea what to expect when I stood at my booth in April 2014. My first book was ready to meet the world, and I was twitching with a mix of nervousness and excitement. (Okay, it was panic and elation.) What I couldn't figure out was why in the world people would want to even talk to me. What were they thinking? As I scheduled and attended more and more events and book signings, I noticed patterns in people's behavior. The more I studied people's behavior, the better I understood the patterns and the better I did at managing both the situation and my own expectations.

BROWSERS

The Browser goes out for the day with no intention of committing to anything. Browsers will engage, smile, listen intently, but they won't buy today. Whether it's because they are on a budget, don't feel like carrying anything heavy, or need a day to just wander around with their thoughts, these people most likely won't buy a thing from us no matter what we say or do.

It's easy to think of these people as being a waste of time, but they aren't. Firstly, it's good to have activity going on at our booth or table, particularly if we've had a bit of a dry spell. People will often hang around in the background when we're giving our pitch, listening, trying to figure out whether they should approach and check out the back of the books.

Another thing the Browser gives us is the opportunity to test out revisions of our pitch.

A question I am frequently asked is how to tell if a potential reader is a Browser. While it's hard to tell reliably if a potential reader is any type in particular, I've found that Browsers tend to stand with their feet solidly planted and their hands together in front of them. They keep their distance, almost as if touching the book would create a sense of obligation or pull them out of their "I'm not buying anything" mindset.

NOW-OR-NEVERS

These people come up to our booths, listen to our pitch, and will make a buy decision here and now. Unlike a standard curious person, Now-or-Nevers are either buying today—right here, right now—or not at all. The book is either worthy of their attention, or it's not. The author is right there in front of them, so what better time to make such a decision?

Often, Now-or-Nevers will ask for comparisons. They pick up our book, examine it, and put it back down. They'll listen to us while they are reading the back of the cover, and then ask us a dozen questions. I find that they will also go quiet at one point, the gears turning behind their eyes. At this point, it's vital to stop talking! They are processing, and anything we say may very well result in us buying our book back.

"Buying your book back" is an expression that means to lose the sale because we keep talking so long that we convince an interested potential reader not to buy our book. This can happen when we give them too much information for them to process or when something we say makes them feel we contradicted something they liked about our book. So, if a Now-or-Never goes quiet, then we do. We stand at the ready, silently. If they're silent for a minute, then we may ask questions to re-engage them *What types of books have you enjoyed recently? Which authors have you read and liked recently? What books do you love to reread?*

On the one hand, we love the certainty of the Now-or-Nevers; on the other hand, once they've made up their mind, there's no recovery. The more we try, the more adamant they can become.

I saw one pushed by an author who refused to let go of the sale and that Now-or-Never turned to the group of curious potential readers at the table. Loud enough for many people to hear, the other author's Now-or-Never said, "Can you believe this guy? His books must be crap, he's pushing them like a used car dealer."

Instead of letting go of one sale to a Now-or-Never, that author lost the interest of a small crowd of potential readers.

A question I often get is how to identify these people. To me, Now-or-Nevers come across as focused and driven. They don't mess around with their shopping: They are on a mission.

DASHERS

Also on a mission, these potential readers are the ones who can't stop. The Dasher will glance in our direction as they approach at high speed, a smile forming on their faces. Our pulse accelerates, and we lean forward as they come within range of our voice. We prepare to invite them with warm words and a friendly gesture when they throw up a hand of protest. Along with the palm-out hand comes some abrupt explanation about why they won't be slowing down. "Heading to the bathroom" and "I've got a kid's birthday party in fifteen minutes" are the two most common statements I get from Dashers as they speed past.

For a long time, I thought there was nothing I could do. These people were in a rush and clearly didn't have time beyond a few quick words. However, they did engage with me. So how could I engage productively within that Dasher's tight time constraint?

Then I looked at my bookmarks. Like any good give-away item, my bookmarks had several key pieces of information: my pen name, the book and series titles I was promoting, a one-line description that identified the book and series genre, my URL, and places where a potential reader could purchase my books. On one useful little bookmark was everything I needed to engage with Dashers.

I had an idea: I would keep a few bookmarks in hand the next time I did a signing. When I spotted a Dasher about to whiz by, I would put out a bookmark and say, "I'd love to tell you about my books sometime."

A funny thing happened when I did that.

About ten percent of the Dashers looked at the bookmark and stopped in front of me. Instead of a quick excuse in my direction, they fired off a quick question directly at me. They asked about my book's reading level and target age, or some other book-related topic that was on their minds. I responded quickly, knowing my engagement time with the Dasher was limited. Half the time, they bought a book and moved on.

About twenty-percent of the Dashers waved me away and went on. No harm, no foul. That's what was happening already.

Fifty percent of the Dashers took the bookmark and didn't give it a second look. When they had the time to check out what they had gotten from the store or the fair or the convention, however, my bookmark was there with them instead of still on my signing table.

The final twenty percent of the Dashers actually came back about ten minutes later, after they did whatever was so critical. A few kept looking at the time, but they felt absolutely compelled to learn more about my books.

None of them, not one, resented me offering my bookmark. Being prepared and adapting to the Dashers' extremely limited window of time to engage with me worked.

If a Dasher does stop for us, they may appear rather anxious. Maybe they are checking the time repeatedly; maybe they are fidgeting. We should respect that any stopped Dashers are caught between their desire to learn more about our book and the need to get their mission done. This means we need to be quick, clear, and a bit extra warm and friendly to emotionally reward them for the time investment they are making. Practicing brief and good-natured replies to questions and learning to complete transactions rapidly helps us to engage Dashers. It's worth investing that time, too. I've had people speeding by, do a sharp one-eighty after I offer a bookmark, and depart with an armful of books two minutes later.

The lesson of the Dasher is that we don't have to pitch our books to every potential reader who streams past us. So many pass by our signing table, especially at conventions. If we try to pitch manically to everyone, then no one will feel special. Most will be dissuaded from engaging with us. We'll be tuned out like a constantly repeated commercial. If we skip a person, or skip two, then we should be fine. Our specific potential readers' ears will perk up overhearing what personally interests them, and they'll engage us.

BOOMERANGS

These people can be standing at our booth, looking excited and eager, maybe even clutching our book. Then, all of a sudden, they will put the book down and walk away! It can be immensely frustrating if we don't understand what's going on. Boomerangs are analytical thinkers; they are rarely impulsive and far more methodical in their decisions and choices, particularly when it comes to something new. After listening to our pitch, and reading the backs of our books, they need time to have their inner debate.

That debate often includes a lot of questions like: "Is this the best time and price?", "Do I have the funds right now?", "Do I want a signed copy?", "Is this an impulse buy? If so, will I regret it?", "Do I have room in my library?", "Do I have time to read it with the long reading queue I already have?", "Will I be insulting this person if I don't buy exactly right now?"

Sometimes Boomerangs will keep coming back to the booth, asking one more question, or rereading the back of the book again. Their return is a great sign. Sometimes I offer a gentle nudge like, "I'd be happy to sign a copy for you." That's as close to trying to sell them a book as I'll come, and I rarely do that.

If we try to push or pressure Boomerangs at a bookstore signing, they'll take our book and abandon it in the store. Boomerangs need time apart from us to settle themselves internally with the idea of buying the book. Maybe they have a mountain of to-be-read books and are trying to figure out if our book would go at the top or if our book would only take up shelf space over the next three months if they bought it now.

Boomerangs, however, are the ones most likely to pick up our book a day, a week, or even a month later. Because Boomerangs are analytical, they will continue to think about it after we've accepted that they chose not to buy our books.

I didn't realize this was a possibility until I happened to be in a big box bookstore a few days after a book signing. A woman I recognized from the signing event came in, walked directly past me, picked up a copy of my book (still not noticing me!), and then headed straight to the cashier. I couldn't believe she'd only come in to get my book, but there it was—the truth right before my very eyes.

Remember, if the person you're talking to seems all excited, and you're getting excited because a sale looks imminent, only for them to pull away, don't be disappointed. They may very well be a Boomerang.

EAR WORMS

For the longest time, I couldn't figure out this certain type of potential reader. They would show up and listen intently. Their eyes and face revealed they were excited, but their hands stayed in their pockets, and they rarely moved to pick up my books. If they looked at the backs of my books, it was a casual once-over and I couldn't tell if they were humoring me or teasing me. The weirder thing was that these indecipherable types would socially engage with me. We would laugh, talk about books, chat about many other subjects, and then they would move on. I wondered if these people were just taunting me, or if I was missing something about the rules of engagement with this type of potential reader.

Then one day at a comic book convention, about an hour after talking with one of these mysterious types of people, one of them showed up with six friends. "This is the amazing author I was telling you guys about. You'd love his books. Buy them."

To my astonishment, the friends didn't ask me a damn thing. They just picked up the books, read the backs, and then bought the books.

That strange and wondrous person was an Ear Worm.

Ear Worms are networkers and influencers. They fully engage, talking to us and collecting a story to share with others—a bit of social currency, as I like to call it. With that social currency, an Ear Worm distributes it to a broader group. Some Ear Worms extend their influence on social media; others, directly in person.

When I thought about it, I realized that I've got a few in my cadre of friends. An Ear Worm is the person who announces, "Have I got a story for you!" and then tells their riveting personal encounter to everyone present. An Ear Worm isn't trying to sell us something; they are sharing an engaging story with you. In doing that, we listeners are influenced by Ear Worms' judgments. The more we've found this person to be accurate in the past, then the greater this person's credibility in the present, and the farther their influence spreads in the future as we tell others what Ear Worms told us.

A good Ear Worm is invaluable. If that Ear Worm comes away with a wonderful story about our encounter after meeting us, then the story will have entertainment value and will be worth sharing. Sometimes the story will lie dormant until the next time they see you. Then they'll drag a friend over and start a conversation between you.

Ear Worms are amazing allies when we're building our author brands and extending our author reach. They're also a treasure for every engagement-focused author, so we want those Ear Worms to walk away with a great story every time we cross paths with one.

CASTAWAYS

Have you ever seen someone lingering around, looking lost? These are the people waiting for their friends, or perhaps their spouse, to finish whatever those friends or that spouse has come to do. That other person could be hunting for a specific book in a different part of the store or could be checking out specific vendor booths at a convention just before heading home. Whatever errand or activity that other person has in mind, the Castaway has decided to opt out.

Castaways aren't looking for a book. They're not even thinking about themselves. They are simply trying to kill time. Castaways are easy enough to spot. Normally, we wouldn't call over someone who's not a potential reader, but if we have no one at our booth, then we could help them and ourselves at the same time.

There's a funny rule about having a busy table: The more people we have at our table, the more people are likely to come over to see what all the excitement's about. If we have no one at our table, and people are just walking by and ignoring us, then potential readers are less likely to come over.

Enter the value of the Castaways. Their presence at our booth as we engage with them might be all we need to seed interest in our books and grow our crowd attention again.

When we reach out to a Castaway, it's very common for them to offer a dismissive wave. They may explain they're just waiting for their daughter, or their wife, or their husband. Then they usually follow that up by explaining that they don't read the kind of book we write or that they don't read at all.

Once the Castaway has explained why they believe it's a waste of my time, I respond, "I get that. How about I entertain you for two minutes? It'll give me some extra practice."

After thinking about it for a few seconds, they usually shrug and either gesture for me to go ahead, or say something like, "Okay, if you want to. Knock yourself out."

I then proceed to give them my book pitch, my attention shifting every now and then to see if I can draw in a potential reader with a "Would you like to hear about the books too?"

Often, the Castaway will get into it as well. They'll even draw in potential readers, engaging them by throwing in an, "Actually, these sound pretty good. They aren't my thing, but you might like them."

They'll then sometimes step aside to make room for that potential reader. If that person they drew to our table shows interest, then they'll often offer us a friendly wink and leave.

Every now and then, the Castaway leaves only to return with the person or people they were with. As if by magic, our Castaway transforms into an Ear Worm. On rare occasion, the Castaway realizes that someone in their life would love our, and they buy it as a gift. The goal with Castaways is to get us pitching again, get ourselves back into a positive mindset, and get potential readers to notice there's interest at our table.

TIME EATER

I am a huge proponent of making time for fans, potential readers, and fellow writers. I strongly believe in being the mentor we all wish we'd found earlier in life. With that said, we always need to be aware that when we are at our table, we're working. In the same way we limit our socializing time at work in favor of paying attention to customers, so do we here.

Time Eaters are out to socialize. They will talk to us until the cows come home, leave again, and return. Some of them are lonely, some may be excited to talk to anyone about writing. The issue with Time Eaters isn't answering some questions; it's about appearing unavailable to passersby. When we chat with people casually, our body language usually communicates to other people that we are busy. It doesn't physically block people from approaching, but it creates a hindrance that they would need to overcome, like driving uphill. We want to be inviting and ready to engage them, making it as easy as coasting downhill.

Some of the worst culprits for Time Eaters are acquaintances. Some are well-meaning yet don't realize what we're doing is work. For them, all we do is tell them: "Can I chat with you later? I see some potential readers about." Most of the time, our friends will move on. But then there are the other ones, who simply don't accept what we're doing as work and will push back against subtle statements. With them I've found I've had to be rather direct. "I'm working, I'll talk with you some other time. Have a great day." And if they don't take that hint, I get really direct.

For most people, the following work as polite ways to disengage:
- "It's been great talking with you. Have a good remainder of your day."
- "All the best with that endeavor (or writing or surgery)."
- "I appreciate you stopping by; have a good one."

Most people will get the message. Sometimes, it requires us to be more direct: "I need to get back to focusing on potential customers and readers (or work). Have a great day, enjoy the store (or show)." Those that remain may very well be the next type we're tackling: the Booth Barnacle.

BOOTH BARNACLES

The Booth Barnacle is a Time Eater who knows we are trying to get rid of them and refuses to go. The more we encourage them to leave, the more they may inch towards the table or start leaning over it. They are challenging us over what is rightfully our turf.

Booth Barnacles don't want to leave until they've decided they're done, and they enjoy our anxiety along the way. I've had some start loudly quoting Bible verses whenever I ask them to leave. Others will give me a snide smirk and just shift subjects.

Not all of us are comfortable with pushing back, being loud, and being assertive. This is something that we need to incorporate into our Author Persona, and the way I like to think of it as defending my place and my space as an author. These people don't respond reasonably to logic or polite words, so they need something stronger. Here are a few strategies I use to get these people to disengage, after I've tried being direct:

- If someone else is walking by, then we step towards that potential reader and offer our opener. When we start talking with another person, 9 times out of 10, the Barnacle will give up and leave.

- If we're at a bookstore, we can go and speak to a staff member and ask them to remove the person. We are a guest in the store, and that means they are there to support us.

- If we're at a convention, we can turn to our booth neighbor and ask, "How do you get people like this to leave?"

- We can place our hands on the table, lean forward, and look down at the table as we draw in a deep breath. Then we look up at the person, with a burning glare, and tell them: "Please leave."

- A good friend of mine has a bold solution. He will start frantically shooing the person away, yelling, "Move along, Looky-loo! Move along!" Not something I could see myself doing, but it works for him.

- If all else fails, we can always lean on the classic out: We go to the washroom.

Because we are in public, however we act can be taken out of context and haunt us. While we always act sincerely and with integrity, we should never compromise our own safety. Therefore, we remain aware of the situation and the location we are in.

Remember our Author Persona is armor, so we should be as assertive as we need to be.

NOT-HELPERS

These are those friends, acquaintances, and rare strangers, who show up and install themselves at our table and jump in on our customer pitches. I've had Not-Helpers try to assist me a few times, and it is very cringeworthy. Several times they have cost me sales.

This is about boundaries. We need to be crystal clear about those signing table helpers who we've officially chosen and those who we have not. Other than for multi-day comic book conventions, I rarely have official helpers with me. Even then, my official helpers are present on the busiest days, during the busiest hours. I walk through the rules with my official helpers, and they respect me as a professional author and my signing booth rules:

- Engaging potential readers is our priority, not socializing. Personal conversations need to end when people are approaching.
- I am the lead. If my helper started talking with someone and I step in, then they are to look for someone else to talk to or to help.
- We never, ever, bully or hard-sell anyone.

In my early days, I was uncomfortable with asking unexpected helpers to move on. Part of me felt like I could use all the help I could get; at the same time, these volunteers often made me really uncomfortable. I came to realize that those Not-Helpers were well-meaning and that I needed to own my author appearance and to control my booth space. It has to be my way or no way, however non-optimal others might see it as being.

It's one thing to have a fan, friend, or satisfied reader share a friendly interjection or an impromptu review with a potential reader, but it's another matter for those folks to jump in every time a new potential reader shows up. The first scenario is okay, even desirable; the second scenario is not okay. Often it takes little more than telling them that we need them to move on.

JEALOUS HOSTILES

I've been told that everyone has a story or a book in them. That's wonderful—until those people become aggressively competitive at our book signing table. Either at the end of our pitch or in the middle, these Jealous Hostiles will say, "I've got a better story than that."

They then proceed to tell us about their story. While I'm all for talking about writing, publishing, and marketing with fellow writers, Jealous Hostiles aren't up for shop-talk or picking up copies of our books to read. They wish to feel superior at our expense, and there's never room for that at our signing table.

Once I've clued into the fact that I'm dealing with a Jealous Hostile, I end it. I'll usually put a hand up and say something along the lines of this: "This isn't a contest. If you're not interested in my stuff, no worries. Have a great day," or "I'm working my table, not up for swapping stories. Thank you."

Jealous Hostiles aren't usually looking for a fight, so being firm and clear with them can help them realize what they're doing. On rare occasion, we can transition this to a fruitful conversation. More often than not, it's best to just see them on their ways.

ANGRY JERKS

Some people act like they're searching for a nemesis, and we're on their short list of interview candidates. These Angry Jerks show up at our table with an axe to grind, and they mean to make themselves memorable. They are verbally abusive and unwilling to hear reason—or even have their opinions respectfully acknowledged.

It's as if Angry Jerks want to spread their bitter rage like a disease. Our author brand (which we've developed using our Author Persona, our reach, and our books) seems to enrage them; they act like they want our author brand to get sick and die. They try to pass their anger to us, so we'll infect our fans, friends, family, and potential readers. As if hoping all of those people will infect others with hatred toward our author brand, Angry Jerks seem obsessed to be the reason we lose our writing careers.

While I and many other authors have been fortunate to have had rare face-to-face encounters with Angry Jerks, I have a friend who became the nemesis of an Angry Jerk. This hostile person still occasionally shows up at my friend's public presentations just to disrupt things.

My most memorable Angry Jerk encounter was at a comic book convention. This Angry Jerk had committed to being an anti-fan of mine. While he was aggressive about his anti-fandom on social media, he had never approached me in person. This time, he attended a talk I'd given that day then followed me back to my book signing table in a group of people. When we arrived, he tried to make a scene.

Now, I admit I engaged this Angry Jerk. I tried to change our relationship only because I was already comfortable in my own Author Persona and felt it was worth it. Even then, it was difficult and delicate work to engage this fury-filled person.

Because Angry Jerks use confrontation to create chaos, I recommend dealing with these people in the same way we would the undesirable Jealous Hostiles or Booth Barnacles. When we take a firm stance and disengage undesirables with purpose, we gain the experience and the confidence to make our book signing areas a pleasant place for potential readers.

SUMMING IT UP

Too many times I've heard an author say something nasty as a person leaves their table without a book in hand, not realizing what I had: That person was a Boomerang and would have come back—if they hadn't also heard the nasty thing the author had said about them. It baffles me that they don't consider that type of unprofessional behavior can convert a Boomerang into a negative Ear Worm (an anti-fan blabbermouth) or even an Angry Jerk (an anti-fan aggressor). We, as authors, should always keep in mind that reach doesn't just build our author brand; it can dismantle it.

Putting ourselves out there is an emotional roller coaster. Every author appearance has its highs—like when we have several potential readers in a row all love our book and buy copies—and every author appearance has its lows—like when no one is around to hear our pitch, or worse, everyone we've spoken to is uninterested in our books. Knowing the different types of people we'll meet, both welcome and undesirable, can help us fight off that sense we're wasting our time or aren't good at what we're doing. More important, we improve at engagement when we acknowledge the value in these different types of people—both welcome and undesirable.

We are there to get the word of our story out, to be an evangelist for our works. As engagement-focused authors we should measure our success by how many people we speak to about our books, and not how many books we signed then sold from our table. (This is much easier said than done, which my wife constantly reminds me when I'm down.)

Different venues, different times of year, and the weather all affect the number and types of people that come our way. The best thing we can do is be prepared to make the best of whatever opportunity is before us. After all, there's nothing like packing up to go home and looking up to see an Ear Worm approaching, trailing a half-dozen friends behind them, jumping up and down while announcing loudly enough to draw strangers' curiosity: "These are the books I was telling you about!"

—9—

CRITICAL THING #4:
FACING THE NUMBERS

Some authors throw their hands up when it comes to numbers. Some say that numbers are irrelevant and that it's all about story. I wish that was true, but it's not, especially in the realm of independently published, or indie, authors.

If we're spending money on our books without the remotest desire to at least break even, then writing and publishing and marketing books is a hobby—and that's fine. I'm talking about turning writing and publishing books into our business and our careers—which means, at the very least, we want to break even as we work toward financial independence through writing.

My own goal is always to have my previous book at least pay for the editing, cover, and initial print run of my next book. If I do that, then I'm content. In order to do that though, I need treat my writing career like a business. I have to pay attention to the numbers.

For some, this makes sense at the outset. For others, the realization that the costs of things are important hits them at a delicate moment. It's art, right? All is fine in the name of art, isn't it?

Let's imagine we're packing up from a signing or event, happy with the day of sales and the number of people we reached. We lift the empty plastic bag that was brimming with buttons when we started that morning. That empty bag represents all the people who stopped by and now have a souvenir to show off as they talk to others about meeting us. Those buttons are out there extending our reach. That's a wonderful thought—isn't it?

Then an uncomfortable realization surfaces. Each one of the buttons cost fifty cents, and that bag held a hundred just this morning. Fifty dollars just walked out that door (wait, what was shipping on those, again?), and this empty bag means we need more buttons before our next scheduled book signing. How much extra will a rush job on buttons cost? Are they worth it?

Let's look at those sales and see if those buttons paid off. It was a good day, right? And when we look at the numbers, we see that we just spent an entire day away from our family so we could actually lose money. Gut punch.

How did this happen?

We need to break everything down and build up an understanding of our costs. It's never too late to start.

Understanding Book Costs

There are several elements to understanding how much your book truly costs you and what you should price it at.

Hardcover, or Not Hardcover—That Is the Question

Like many people, I really like the look and feel of hardcovers, but does my preference make business sense? Here are a few points to consider:

- Greater Cost. Hardcovers cost more, and retail for more. They also require more effort (dust jacket). Printing them only makes sense when doing volume, otherwise the cost is too high.

- Personal Taste. Not everyone likes hardcovers more than paperbacks. I've learned that a lot of people who like to read in bed don't like how hardcovers feel in their laps.

- No right answer. We will never satisfy everyone. We need to think of our potential readers, the venues where we will be doing signings, and what will likely sell at those events. It doesn't matter what we want, it's what they want. Ego can be our undoing if we're not careful.

There are other points we can consider, like having the ability to change the dust-jacket—which is cheaper than reprinting paperbacks—and the ability to offer bonus content in the hardcover. In the end, it seems to boil down to cost and accepting not everyone likes or buys hardcovers.

Cost Per Individual Book

How much does that printed copy of our book really cost us?

Say we have an event coming up. Instead of the usual $19.99 price tag, we'd like to price it at $15. Would we lose money?

$15 sales price - cost per copy = profit per copy

The most obvious place to start calculating that cost per copy is our print run. We figure we'll sell thirty books at the event, maybe as many as fifty. That means we'll need a quote from our book printer, which could be:

- Amazon (KDP) Paperback
- Lulu
- Ingram Spark
- Print Raven
- Our local print shop

But how many should we order? As career authors, we often don't have much money available, and we definitely don't want to be stuck with a basement or storage unit full of books.

The Art of Book Ordering

My own book printer quotes me for 50, 100, and 250 books. On the surface, my cost per copy looks like the following:

50 books cost $600 = $12 each
100 books cost $900 = $9 each
250 books cost $1750 = $7 each

Very often printers have a tipping point at which the cost of paper and printing drops. Printers offer customers a profound price drop per copy, or a price break, when they reach their magic number. In a recent quote I received, my printer's magic number was 1,250 copies. If I printed fewer than that number, the prices were good; at 1,250 and more, the price per unit was significantly less:

1,250 books cost $2187.50 = $1.75 each

However, over-buying is worse than underbuying for a couple of reasons. First, over-buying limits how soon we could tweak the back-of-the-book blurb. Second, investing a lot of money up front is risky

We never know how well a book's going to do. Even if one of our books is fantastically popular, that's no guarantee any other book we publish will do well. Personally, I find there's way more joy in ordering more copies than chipping away at a huge pile in a storage locker. For example, one of my paperback books has been reprinted five times, each print run has been between one and three thousand, which is great. I started smaller and built up. However, when I released a different book, and did it as a hardcover, printing one thousand five hundred of them left me with a lot of heavy, bulk books to store. Why? The former sells fast and the latter sells slowly.

We might think you're going to sell thirty to fifty books at the event we're planning for, but do we have one or more potential events on the horizon? Assuming we have scheduled one other event, let's order 100 books for our exercise:

100 books cost $900 = $9 each

From our earlier decision to price our books at $15 per copy, that means:

$15 sales price - $9 cost per copy = $6 profit per copy

Selling nine copies means we've paid for that bag of giveaway buttons and have four dollars left over to get a celebratory hot drink on the way out. And we just sold between thirty and fifty copies!

Not So Fast

In the previous section, I said "on the surface" regarding costs per book copy because we need to consider several things when figuring out our actual book costs.

Damage

It's sadly normal, but book damage is just part of print publishing. For me, around 1-3% of my print run is in some way damaged, and I end up giving those copies away. Sometimes the printer misprints a few copies. Sometimes the shipper damages copies. Sometimes I accidentally mis-sign a book (To George—dangit, I meant Jerome!) or drop a book in a puddle.

On one occasion I had a box come apart in a lake of parking lot as I went from my car to the venue. Fortunately I only lost a half-dozen books, and this is rare.

Let's assume three copies from our print run are lost to damage:

100 books - 3 damaged = 97 good copies

Reviews and Gifts

Also normal, though not sad, giving away free copies is also part of print publishing. Either in exchange for an honest review or because we had two minutes to scare up a birthday gift before we get in the car, we must assume copies are given to reviewers and friends.

97 books - 3 giveaways = 94 good copies

Without removing a copy for our own personal library, or anything else, let's see where this leaves us. Out of the 100 copies we bought, we have 94 copies that are available to be sold. That means our cost per book is not no longer $9 each:

94 books cost $900 = $9.57 each

$15 sales price - $9.57 cost per copy = $5.43 profit per copy

So now ten copies sold pays for that bag of giveaway buttons and our celebratory drink for a great day of thirty to fifty copies sold. That bag of buttons still isn't a loss for the day.

BUT WAIT, we're not done yet!

The Choice

Remember that $300 we spent on an eye-catching cover and the $1,200 we spent on editing, proofreading, and formatting? Are we going to ignore those, or are we going to make a business decision?

Cover, editing, and formatting costs are especially tricky. Half of the independently published, or indie, authors I know just ignore this and move on. There are a few who are on the other end of the spectrum. They factor in annual insurance costs, upgrading their laptop and other materials every three years, and so on. Account for what we're comfortable with.

For the purpose of our exercise, let's assume that over the next two years, we will sell 500 print copies of our book at book signings and other author appearance events. The rest of our sales will be from online sales and direct print-on-demand sales. That $300 + $1,200 is going to be spread over 500 copies of the book (five print runs). Where does that leave us?

$1,200 for editing + $300 for a cover = $1500 supplemental costs

$1,500 supplemental costs / 500 copies = $3 in supplemental costs per book copy

$9.57 print cost per good copy + $3 supplemental costs per first 500 good copies = $12.57 cost per first 500 good copies

I personally like to go one step further and include marketing materials' costs as part of my book cost. Therefore, I include the price of any new banners, bookmarks, and giveaways in my per-copy cost. I expect all of those to get paid off over that my initial print run. We don't have to do this, but it's a choice you we should actively make. For our example, we can ignore our marketing materials' costs. However, we always want to keep receipts and records of every marketing expense from the start. We'll need them to factor them in with the rest of our real-world costs once when we're comfortable. Also, I highly recommend getting an account, or at least a bookkeeper, who is familiar with authors and heeding their advice. I'm many things, but an expert in accounting is not one of them.

Mind the Margins

What first looked like a nice $9 per book cost for 100 copies, ended up being $12.57 per book with only ninety-four available to be sold after stock losses. So what does this really mean if we still want to sell that first print run for $15 per copy?

$15 sales price per copy - $12.57 cost per copy = $2.43 profit per copy

Therefore we're not making $6 per book or even $5.43, but rather $2.43 for five print runs—plus part of a sixth one? That means to pay for that bag of buttons, now, we have to sell twenty-one copies. Our day of thirty to fifty sales isn't looking so great any more when we have 450 or more sales to go to get out from under those supplemental costs.

That is, if we never plan to sell our books on consignment at bookstores.

Of Stores and Margins

If we're at a convention or book fair, we have a cost for reserving table, or renting a space. Being in a store is a different situation, as there's (usually) no cost for the table. There is, however, a percentage of sales as a commission.

If we're selling books through an independent bookstore, they usually require a minimum of 40% discount off the cover price as their cost. For our example, Bookstore A is offering a 40% consignment deal:

Bookstore A

*$15 cover price * 40% = $6 Bookstore A discount/profit*

$15 cover price - $6 discount/profit = $9 sales price to Bookstore A

That means if we're still planning to sell it for $15, they will buy it from us for $9. That allows them to make up to $6 per book. (They'll make less if they put it on sale.)

However, we may notice based on our buying of 100 books, and our actual costs, what that would mean that if we did a signing event at a store like this:

$9 sales price to Bookstore A - $12.57 cost per first 500 good copies = (-3.57) profit

Other stores, particularly bigger stores, will require a 45% discount if we're doing consignment, and potentially as much as a 55% discount:

Big Bookstore B

*$15 cover price * 45% = $6.75 Big Bookstore B discount/profit*

$15 cover price - $6.75 discount/profit = $8.25 sales price to Big Bookstore B

$8.25 sales price to Big Bookstore B - $12.57 cost per first 500 good copies = (-$4.32) profit

Big Box Bookstore C

*$15 cover price * 55% = $8.25 Big Box Bookstore C discount/profit*

$15 cover price - $8.25 discount/profit = $6.75 sales price to Big Box Bookstore C

$6.75 sales price to Big Box Bookstore C - $12.57 cost per first 500 good copies = (-$5.82) profit

Despite what appear to be incredible losses, having our books in a bookstore means that potential readers can see them any time that bookstore is open. Instead of just three days per year at a single weekend convention or fair, our books are on display three hundred (or more) days per year.

A great day of sales turning into a loss over $50 in giveaway buttons seems pretty small when our margins can vary so much from situation to situation.

Numbers Don't Lie

We should not be scared of numbers, and we should not run around with blinders on. Doing a bit of basic math can help us make the best business decisions. It really is better to know, rather than fear, what the reality is. When we know, we can make the changes that can turn a negative profit margin into a positive one.

Maybe we need to set our book price at $19 or $24 instead of $15. Already printed some books with the lower cover price? Get some stickers made. I had to do that once when I accidentally printed an incorrect book price right on the cover.

Alternatively, we can decide not to list a price on our book. I have some good friends who prefer this strategy, however I've found for me it causes headaches. I've seen readers put off their decision, or made uncomfortable, not knowing how much something is (in a bookstore) or how much of a deal their getting (at an event). That said, this really applies to when we are doing print runs (e.g. 100+ copies, usually from a printing company). This advice differs when we're getting our books printed by a print-on-demand (POD) service.

When dealing with POD, there are a number of factors to take into consideration. For my books, I don't put the price on the back of POD books anymore, and here's why. As a Canadian, I need to monitor the foreign exchange rate (Canadian vs American dollar). Then there's the cost from the printer, which can change without notice. If I need to adjust the price, because I'm now losing money, I don't want to have to change the back cover of the book. Therefore, best to leave it blank. In essence, a print run has a fixed cost whereas dealing with POD has a dynamic one.

For completeness, having a price printed on the back of the book doesn't mean we can't change it. It just means that a store sticker is going to need to be put over top of the book. On a few occasions, a store forgot to do that (or a customer peeled it off), and so some books sold at the incorrect price.

By the way, if you're someone like me who sometimes feels our soul ice up when it comes to accounting stuff, then ask a money-savvy friend to sit with you and help. We all have our strengths, and we all have areas where we need the strength of others. In turn, we can help them in the areas where they need our strength.

Lose the fear. Get the facts. Know where you stand.

THE HIGH PRICE OF GIVEAWAYS

This is the generally part in the story where our beaten-down hero has gotten to their feet and is leaning against the doorframe after winning a ferocious fight. They close their eyes to bask in the warm, soothing light of the sun, and they savor the hard-earned, bitter victory. We relax with our hero. Everything is going to be fine.

The music changes, our stomach churns, and then we see it. A shadow is approaching in the background. The battle isn't over!

In this case, that approaching shadow is book signing giveaways. Specifically, I mean pins, pens, candies, bookmarks, t-shirts, tea cups, buttons—everything we give to people to extend our reach and build our author brand as we promote our Author Personas and our books. I've seen other authors with branded bags, USB keys, and more.

I've seen people come up to my book signing booth, and those of my friends, and ask if pens, candy, or buttons were free. As soon as the reply yes is uttered, these people will clean an author out of giveaways. They take promotional items by the fistful!

It's funny how differently some people behaved when I reply, "You can have one, if you like," or "Not usually, but you know what? Have one."

Nothing is free. Promotional giveaways are a complimentary gift from us to them. We are offering these up for zero cost to the potential reader, but there's a difference between free and complimentary. Everything we give away is marketing dollars that need to be paid back to we through sales. Therefore, we never reply yes when anyone asks if our book signing giveaways are free.

Let's consider those buttons again. In this example, I am having a Book Character Button Giveaway at a book fair or convention table. I have poured my entire bag of buttons into a container and have set it on my table. People can take from the container, but I have decided not to say yes if anyone asks if they're free.

If each button with a picture of one of my characters on it costs me $0.50, and people take 100 of them over the course of a day, that means from whatever net profit I made from book sales (number of books sold * [sold price minus our real cost]), I now need to deduct the $50 that I gave away in character buttons:

*Number of books sold * [sold price - real cost = Gross Profit Per Copy] = Book Sales Gross Profit*

*Book Sales Net Profit - [button real cost * buttons given away] = net profit after Book Character Button Giveaway*

If I made $5 per book (my gross profit per copy) and sold thirty books:

*30 books sold * [$5 net profit per copy] = $150 Book Sales Gross Profit*

A gross profit of $150 sounds good. Now I need to determine how much I actually made after that character button giveaway:

*$0.50 button real cost * 100 buttons given away = $50 Book Character Button Giveaway cost*

$150 Book Sales Gross Profit - [$50 Character Button Giveaway Cost] = $100 net profit after Book Character Button Giveaway

A third of my profit vanished with those character buttons! I feel very fortunate that I had a $5 profit per book, so I walked away with something. If my profit per book had been less than $1.50, then I would have lost money at what would have looked like a successful signing. That character button giveaway would have meant I spent the entire day away from my family and lost money.

I probably shouldn't have let people take as many as they wanted. Going forward, I knew I'd need to be more decisive and assertive. The next time, I tried to limit people to one character button with each book purchase instead of setting them in a basket for anyone to take. Of course, I gave some away here and there for promotion, but I was a lot more conscious of when and where.

The lesson of promotional giveaways is that letting people take what they want can leave us broke.

There are often ways to reduce the costs of our giveaways with a bit of extra effort and thought. Let's take bookmarks as an example. We can find bookmarks from online printers for as little as twenty-five cents per bookmark, in volume. Yet I pay seven and a half cents per bookmark.

How do I do that?

One day, my wife noticed that rack cards are about the size of two bookmarks, as shown here. They're also made of a sturdier material than usual bookmarks, which is great. A rack card is like a postcard, only bigger.

Better yet, whereas the official bookmarks that were being sold were small enough to be lost in a book, rack cards were long enough to always stick out—which people loved.

A printed rack card can be as inexpensive as $0.15 per card if purchased in volume or on sale. Cut them in half, and we've got 2 bookmarks for that $0.15, or $0.075 per bookmark. This required the investment of a $100 cutter, however.

Let's do the math for 500 bookmarks to see if we will break even on the investment of the cutter with 500 bookmarks. We're going to ignore shipping costs and taxes for simplicity. In the example below, the rack cards are the top-quality kind with premium thickness and a glossy front.

500 bookmarks cost $270 = $0.54 per printer-cut bookmark
250 Rack cards cost $75 = $0.30 per rack card

If we divide each rack card in two to make 500 bookmarks:

$0.30 per rack card / 2 bookmarks = $0.15 per rack-card bookmark

Fifteen cents per premium, extra-large bookmark is great compared to fifty-four cents for a premium regular bookmark. Let's now add the cost of our cutter to see if it's worth it for those first 500 rack cards:
$75 for 500 rack-card bookmarks + $100 cutter = $175 for first 500 rack-card bookmarks
$175 / 500 rack-card bookmarks = $0.35 per rack-card bookmark

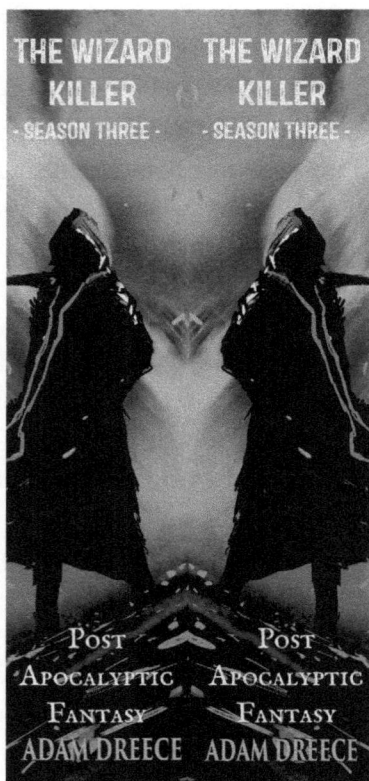

Let's compare:

$0.54 per printer-cut bookmark (every order)
$0.35 per premium rack-card bookmarks (first order)
$0.15 per premium rack-card bookmark (every order thereafter)

So instead of an order of 500 bookmarks, we could order 250 rack cards and a cutter, cut the rack cards into bookmarks ourselves, and do more than break even. Also, the next time we're ordering bookmarks, we'll come out ahead taking the rack card approach.

Whether it's buttons, bookmarks, or any other form of giveaway, we need to be conscious of the costs. Is the book signing souvenir going to be effective in getting people to remember our books and look us up, or will they just come over to take the free things and forget about us?

MEASURING YOUR SUCCESS

Very often we can get caught up in the moment and intuit that things are or aren't going well. An essential part to successful book signings is keeping track of our sales numbers so that we can be honest with ourselves. Every now and then, our feelings can be wildly off.

Success is a funny word. If we set out to sell ten books and sell twenty, that most likely feels like a success. What happens if we only sell five? Objectively, we might say it was a failure. But what if only one person came in the store that day, and we impressed them so much, they bought five copies? That would make it feel a bit different, wouldn't it? I've had times when I expected to sell fifty copies, but I sold thirty, and I was down until a store manager stated how even the best authors they'd had in lately struggled to sell twenty copies.

One of the things that really helped me manage how many books I needed to order was a spreadsheet of all the author and book signing events I attended. In that spreadsheet, I recorded beforehand my best guesses of how many books I felt I would sell at the bookstore signing or book fair or conference. I had another column for how many books I did sell at the event, as well as columns with the date and the event's name. I had a third column which calculated the difference between my estimate (best guess) and how many I sold. That allowed me to check my feelings against real numbers.

Date	Event Name	Est. Sales - Book 1	Act. Sales - Book 1	Actual vs Guess
Feb 1, 2019	ABC Store signing	12	15	+3

You can download a sample spreadsheet from AdamDreece.com/5ct.

Here's what each of the columns represents:

• Column 1 - Date. This is the date that the event is going to take place. Sometimes the time of year makes all of the difference, so knowing the when of an event is as important as knowing the where.

• Column 2 - Event Name. If I'm at a comic book convention, I put its name. If I'm signing books at a big box store, I record the name of the store and its general location, e.g. Book Lovers on 5th Ave. Some big box bookstore locations are busier than others at different times of the week or month or year, so that affects how many potential readers could stop at my signing table.

• Column 3 - Estimated Sales of Book 1. This is the number of copies of Book 1 that I think I might sell. It's my best guess, given everything I know. If I know nothing, then I still put something. Being wrong doesn't matter.

• Column 4 - Actual Sales of Book 1. This is the number of copies of Book 1 that I actually sold, entered after the event.

• Column 5 - Actual vs Guess. This is the number of actual sales minus the estimated sales of Book 1. If the result is positive, it means I underestimated how many I would sell (sold more). If it's zero, it means I guessed perfectly, which is what we strive for because this will help us manage inventory better. If it's negative, that means I overestimated how many I would sell on that day.

The more books I wrote, the more columns I added to track each published title. After my estimated, actual, and delta sales columns for one book title, I added those same three columns for my next book title. Doing that kept it all organized, so I could see which books and series sold better when and where. I went from feeling fear to knowing facts—and I was able to use my spreadsheet to get the best price per book for my print runs.

The first year I maintained this spreadsheet, it helped me get a bit better at estimating sales as the year went on. The second year was when it really paid off. I'd done at least two signings at each of the bookstores in my general area, so that gave me a much better idea of how many copies of my book I was likely to sell at each location. My estimates and actual sales were pretty close, with exceptions telling me whether I was getting better (which it was in a few cases) or if it was a fluke (positive or negative).

I then enhanced the spreadsheet to provide me an auto-updating total of how many books I needed to have in inventory for certain event dates. For example, if I accepted an unexpected school talk two months before a big convention and sold a lot there, I could put in the day's sales and see immediately that I had to order more books, or my convention inventory would likely be short.

By year three, I stopped scheduling book signings at stores where I decided I chronically underperformed. Having this data also allowed me to see sales flukes, such as a store where I usually had good sales, having an off day.

Identifying Important Trends

One of the most valuable things my spreadsheet showed me as I kept track of these basic numbers was when I started to sell fewer copies in Year Three than in Year Two. At first, I thought it was me, and then I realized that book sales had diminished in general across all stores and events. That's when I realized, "Wait, it's not me. People really are spending a lot less." Why? Because my community is a mostly oil-based economy, and people had lost their jobs due to the crash in oil prices.

I also discovered by looking at my data that book sales slumped between May and August—unless I was at large indoor-mall bookstores that allowed me to be visible to the mall's foot traffic, rather than hidden somewhere deep inside the store. By keeping a simple spreadsheet, I was pleasantly surprised by how much I learned about maximizing both my book sales and my sales inventory.

Ordering books ties up money. We don't want to order 2,000 copies if we can only foresee ourselves selling 200 copies in the next year. By keeping track of how we've felt we would do and how we've been doing, we can get a sense how to make the best use of our book signing income.

To that I say we don't have time NOT to face the numbers!

Little lapses turn into career-collapsing catastrophes if we ignore the trends (upward and downward) that affect our writing income. I believe tracking our numbers is really important, so I'm going to do more than just provide that little sample table in the previous section.

Here's what I recommend every author does, because these steps worked for me when I started years ago and still work for me today:

Step One: Set up a simple spreadsheet

Whether we do it in Google Docs, Microsoft Excel, it doesn't matter. We need to track our events, the books we've sold, and the number of copies we estimate we're going to sell. That balance of feelings and figures does so much more than teach us how to estimate sales realistically. With a record, we can see clearly how an amazing or an awful day of sales can signal to us the start of a much bigger trend. If we're aware of the trend, then we can plan wisely to maximize our book sales income or minimize our book sales losses. A maintained spreadsheet means we can still feel great about a book signing day even when our hand-selling figures slip.

To speed things up, download my spreadsheet from here: AdamDreece.com/5ct

Step Two: Keep Track of What We're Selling at Our Event

Whether that means keeping track of every sale through a mobile point-of-sale application or using a pad of paper, we need to keep track of the day's sales. At one point, I created a spreadsheet that I printed out for each event. It had a column for each book I was selling at that event and a row for each sales transaction.

These days, I keep track of every transaction through Square's mobile point-of-sale application. For events like book fairs and conventions, a mobile point-of-sale solution is a must-have in the twenty-first century. Square's Point-of-Sale application has everything I need. I can accept credit and debit card payments with its card-swipe peripheral. I also can record cash and other transactions, so it can keep my daily receipts in order.

Step Three: Capture the Sales Data as Soon as the Event Is Done

If we can't for some reason, then make sure we do record every transaction as soon as we can. The longer we wait, the less likely it becomes that we'll maintain good records. This should take five minutes once we get used to it.

By investing five to six minutes per event, we can start building valuable data. We don't even need to look at it until we're ready. It's just really important that we capture it. The sooner we start down this path, the sooner we'll know what works and what doesn't at the same time we get better at managing our inventory of books.

Summing It Up

Long before I ever wrote my first book, I found myself sitting with a good friend who was emotionally panicked. She had published several New Age books over the years and was working on another one. I asked what was troubling her, and she shared a few of her concerns with me.

She was spending more money on daycare for her son than she was earning from her books and the editing she did on the side.

We knew each other well enough that I felt comfortable asking her if she knew this, and her answer was burned into my soul. With sunken, haunted eyes, she stared at me and said, "I can't think about that. If I think about that, my whole world's going to fall apart. I just have to work more."

I share this story because some of us know the costs we should take into consideration yet don't acknowledge them. Others of us never really thought about it before and choose to become empowered by figuring it out. There's a group of us who are terrified to discover the truth, certain that we're going to be a financial fraud. We fear we'll harm, rather than help, those around us.

My wife regularly tells me that measuring myself as an author in terms of money is wrong. She asserts I need to look at the people's lives that I've touched and the joy I've created. She insists I need to think about the value that my words, as art, have created. It's always challenging for me to really internalize her advice and calm myself down, but she's right.

Now, with a calm mind, I owe it to myself to have an honest understanding of where I'm at and what's happening to me financially. If

I'm spending an entire day at a book signing and earning nothing, that's okay—as long as I know it and it's my consciously active choice.

An author's career is like running a marathon, not a sprint (despite what a lot of indie/self-publishing advice says). Knowing our numbers is important because it puts the power in our hands and helps us be honest with ourselves. That signing that we thought was a complete waste of time might just turn out to have been great—when we look at the numbers.

−10−

CRITICAL THING #5: PRESENTATION IS EVERYTHING

Remember that old saying that you can't judge a book by its cover? It's true. However, we live in such a highly visual era that we can't help ourselves.

Take an app icon on our smart phone for a moment. It's smaller than one inch by one inch, yet at a glance, we can often determine the type of mobile application it is based on its image and colors. We also develop a judgment about its quality and how likely we are to enjoy it. Over the years, software teams have learned to communicate a lot with an icon, and we've learned to understand those images.

Let's go from that less-than-one-inch-by-one-inch icon, and look at a book cover that could be five-and-a-quarter inches by eight inches, or bigger. That's a lot more real estate in which to communicate everything from emotional feel to genre. But why stop there? Now think of a six-foot long table, or a ten-foot-by-ten-foot corner booth? There's much we can communicate, so we need to be smart about how we do it.

When I present on this topic, I always see some stoic faces in the crowd. Those people are sitting with their folded arms and their defensive frowns, quietly arguing to themselves with me that it doesn't matter, or that they aren't subject to such snap judgments. That's when I offer this example:

Suppose we're looking to go out for dinner. We see one restaurant that's well-lit, it's full of people yet not too crowded, and its signage is clear. Its current dinner menu is posted at the door inside an illuminated, enclosed display.

Then there's another restaurant that's dark, it's empty except for wait staff, and we can't make head or tails of its sign. No menu is posted, so we can't even tell what kind of food they serve.

We might go over and peer into the restaurant through its windows, hoping to have our initial concerns washed away by a glimmer of some treasure inside. We may even be bold enough to walk inside and ask the host or hostess to look at a menu. If the restaurant isn't busy, or we don't recognize the restaurant owners, we're a lot more likely to leave. Why? Unless we're feeling particularly adventurous (which lets us overcome our default tendencies) we're going to think of our past experiences. Personally, I've learned by being sick a lot the following days to be highly suspicious of dark and empty restaurants.

Now what if we were strolling an aisle at a book fair looking for new books instead of strolling a street a looking for dinner? What if we were talking about book signing booths instead of restaurants? How willing would you be to go over to a book signing booth where there's an obvious grammar error on the lone badly made sign? Imagine you choose to visit, pick up the book, assuming the mistakes must have been because the author was tired or frantic after something terrible happened to their display signs. Unfortunately, the book has a terrible cover unrelated to the confusing back-cover book summary. Leafing through it, you quickly spot several obvious grammatical errors—including the same one on the booth's sign. Would you buy the book? What are the chances that you'd enjoy the book if you felt particularly adventurous?

Hopefully our perseverance of fighting through mistakes would be rewarded with an excellent story. If it wasn't, then the next time we come across a booth like that, we are more likely to carry on walking. Why? Past experiences.

BRAND WHO?

One of the biggest mistakes fellow authors make is the message they communicate to the public. I've made this mistake myself.

Your table, your booth, whatever you have setup, needs to make a clear statement about what you have to offer.

I've seen some indie authors who have several books to offer but they are hidden under all the promotional material and giveaways of their personal publishing company. Usually this approach is under the misguided belief that it will lend more credibility to the books, but it doesn't. The greatest credibility is given by making the books the star of the show. Potential readers will be impressed with what we really have to offer, not the mask of some publishing company they've never heard of. If we're looking to publish other authors, then we need to be clear what the booth is for and which idea (our books or our publishing company) is going to be dominant. What we want is for people to come to recognize our name, our brand. No matter who publishes our books—maybe we'll have a traditional publisher sometime in the future—we want all of our books to be sought after for the same reason: The reader trusts and loves the types of stories we write. I had to learn this lesson the hard way.

For the first two years I did events, I filled out the vendor forms in my publishing company's name, ADZO Publishing. This made sense as I wanted my company to be invoiced. I didn't see a problem with ADZO Publishing appearing in the list of vendors, if anything, I thought it added some extra credibility!

Imagine how I felt when I kept hearing, time and again, "Oh! You're actually here. We nearly missed you. We couldn't find you in the guide book." For a while, it didn't click in my head. I pointed out that my publishing company was right there, the fan smiled, I smiled, and life went on. But one day a fan said, "I was looking for your name, Adam Dreece. I never remember publisher's names." Huh.

That got me thinking and realizing an obvious thing: what did I really want fans to think of at the end of the book? What an amazing book ADZO Publishing had released? Or what a wonderful story by some guy named Adam Dreece? The answer was painfully clear.

The next time I was signing up I asked if I could be invoiced under one name and in the vendors list as another. The answer? Of course, no problem.

The following year, something awesome happened. At each event, within the first hour of it opening, I had people showing up immediately at my booth. "Found you! Give me what's new!" Fans were finding me.

Fine, we might say, I get it: Don't put my publishing company first. But it's not just that.

Some of us have causes we hold near and dear. When I launched my first book, I had pamphlets for Kids Cancer Care, a charity that helps kids with cancer. I've seen other authors do this too, and we all seem to run into the same problem: People get confused Those people who sell jewelry as well as their books? Same thing. We have to ask ourselves what we are promoting. Is it our literary works or something else? Are we diluting our brand message?

I have some very passionate friends who tell me that they are offering themselves up as artists on that table, not just authors, so they are putting out all of their endeavors. That's fine, but we must be aware of the consequences we face doing that.

My advice is to keep things simple and focused when it comes to our book signing events. We are there to reach new people, sell our books, and to share our imagination, so let's do it!

Over the years, I've tried selling t-shirts and other goods branded with my book covers and whatnot. Whenever I tried, my book sales decreased, my net sales decreased (i.e. the non-book stuff didn't sell all that well), and my potential readers' confusion increased. People could no longer glance my way and immediately register that I was an author making a special book signing appearance. Instead, I looked like one of many general-purpose vendors with lots of things for sale, as well as some books by anyone. When our booth is focused on promoting our books and our author brand, not trying to be a generalized pop-up store, our presence more pronounced and increases the likelihood of getting the right attention quickly. That attention can then be drawn in and the person engaged, and that's a great thing.

To finish, I'd like to add a note about what to do when we write under multiple pseudonyms. Often, I get asked whether or not we should include those books. Unless the Author Personas and the related author brands conflict with each other (for example, children's books about fairness in friendships and true-crime books about serial killers), I say yes.

When it comes to strengthening our author brand at book fairs and comic conventions, focus is key. It's not that nothing else is important, it's that the greater number of distractions, the greater chance you'll lose the passerby. A display that is devoid of unnecessary distractions will draw more people than lower prices. We and our work are the things to put in the spotlight, and we shouldn't be afraid or uncomfortable about it.

A Word on Titles

In the realm of presentation, the title of a book and series are critical pieces of the ensemble. As much as the eye is drawn to the cover image, the mind is drawn to the title. With title and image together, a prospective reader deciphers as much as they can about the book. They figure out whether or not they might like it and decide if they should give our book a more thorough look. Propelled forward by curiosity or repelled by disinterest, a potential reader's reaction to our book and series titles makes our job of drawing them over to engage with us easier or harder. Fortunately, it's something very much under our control.

If we were looking for an emotionally meaty book and saw one called A Sad Adventure beside another called A Journey Through Sorrow, which one would we be more curious about? Most people would be drawn to the latter title for a number of reasons, a key reason being that the words "Journey Through" imply coming out the other side. It promises a complete story arc.

Our book or series titles should never compel us to say in the first seconds of encountering someone, "Don't be put off by the title." To avoid starting from a position of weakness, from a hole we created, it is important to test out our titles.

I've found book signings to be a great opportunity to test out titles and mock covers for future books on people, though social media and my newsletter are my primary avenues. Often, I will create a cover to give it some context—they are unusable covers, but they help set the mood. That said, there's never a guarantee as to how the world will react but testing out titles can help identify any obvious problems.

If we're an indie author, then we address it. There's no reason to live with poor engagement and sales for Snug Gets Loose with its peaceful and pastoral cover, when the story inside is a dark fantasy adventure about recapturing a savage dragon. Change the title and cover to intrigue to readers of the dark fantasy genre, print up a poster of the book with the new title and sell out of that remaining Snug Gets Loose stock.

When we're able to use our Author Persona to engage potential readers at our signing tables and convince them to look beyond our title and cover art, we can control our presentation. When that book leaves our table with that reader, however, we lose that control. When the book is at the bookstore, sitting on the shelf, we have no control. The only things standing up to get noticed is the title, our name, and the cover.

ABOUT THE BOOK COVER

The book cover is a key piece of intrigue and will be communicating a lot to passersby. If an app icon on a phone can tell us several things, a book cover can tell us so much more.

When I launched my first book back in 2014 at a comic convention, I learned a lot about the cover I had selected. I watched people's reactions, and I pushed myself to ask those who I noticed had a strong reaction, both positive and negative. I learned that book covers communicate a lot of different things. I was told the font said fairy-tale but not steampunk, so it didn't communicate the genre properly. I also found out that the cover made men and boys feel uncomfortable buying it for themselves because they felt it was too girly. Some teenagers were put off by the age of the girl on the cover. Worrying that it was too young for them, they had decided to not even give the back of the book a look.

I took all that feedback, chewed on it, and a few months later came out with a new style of cover that ran for the entire series. On the left is my original cover, and on the right the revised one. Note that in the revised one, it's clear that this is a series.

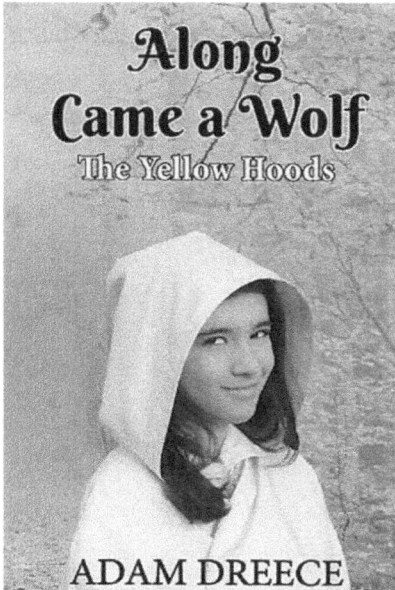

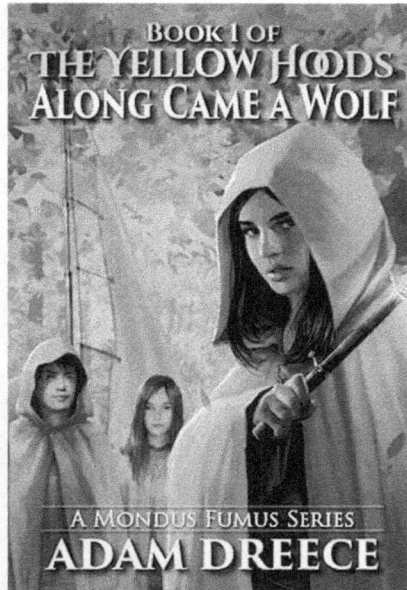

As another example, I discovered that my science fiction novel's audience was more attracted to a very different type of cover than I first thought. Here's how that one changed only to find a split audience. Again, the original on the left and the newer one on the right.

Through engaging readers and potential readers, I learned to vary colors, fonts, and imagery to convey the right messages for different audiences. For example, here's a cover from one of my post-apocalyptic fantasy novels:

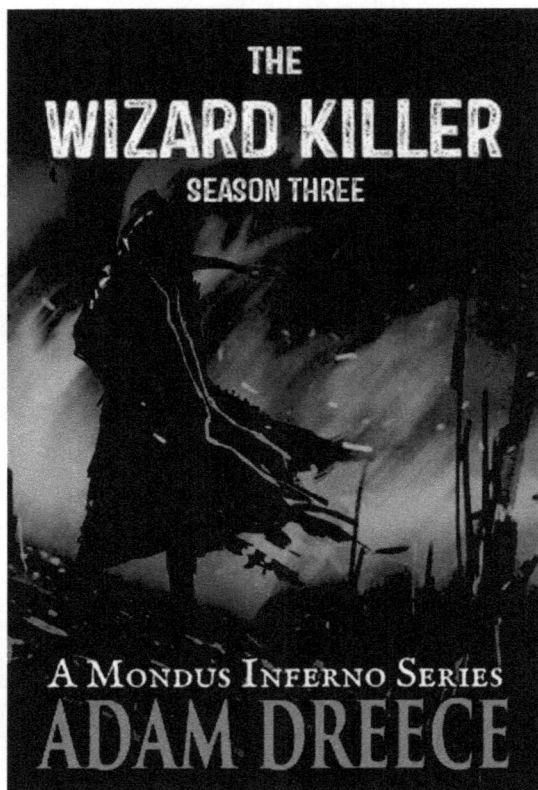

THE
WIZARD KILLER
SEASON THREE

A MONDUS INFERNO SERIES
ADAM DREECE

Someone who is drawn visually to the cover for Along Came a Wolf, may still be visually drawn to the cover for The Wizard Killer, but they'll immediately know not to expect the same type of story.

One of the things that I observed through my many signings is that a lot of potential readers follow a pattern. They'll study the cover of the book while they listen to the pitch; then they'll read the back blurb; and then they'll return to the cover and look at it for a while. It's like they are hunting for the answer to whether they should buy the book, asking themselves questions like: Does this remind me of a book or movie I like? Does the imagery make me feel the way I'd like to feel?

A great book cover for our fantastic story still isn't enough. A single, beautiful book sitting alone on a table, its stunning cover facing the ceiling, isn't capable of enticing people from across a store to come and check it out. We need a display to attract attention, and that means a table laid out to show off our books and banners that know their purpose.

SETTING THE TABLE

It pays dividends to think through your table setup, to learn from others and steal their best ideas. I'm going to cover the three essentials: vertical banners, horizontal banners, and the table top.

Display Essential One: Vertical Banners

When I was preparing my first booth, I couldn't picture what a vertical banner should look like for an author appearance and book signing. My head filled with all manner of doubts about what I should do. I Googled "author banner images" and was presented with all manner of types and styles of vertical banners.

The vertical banner performs a few roles. In a store or at a convention, when customers or attendees are full of energy, they will scan the area to take in their surroundings. Their lines of vision will be high, so the purpose of the vertical banner is to catch that passerby's attention and draw it down to our table. While their eyes sweep down the vertical banner, the mind is absorbing information. With curious images, a book title, and some questions bubbling in their heads, potential readers will notice us and the tempting table display in front of us.

Like a flag flapping above the tree line, a vertical banner introduces potential readers to what we are about and prepares them for us and our book signing table.

To grab attention and draw potential readers to the display at our signing table, our banner should be eye-catching from a distance. Information should be readable from twenty feet away; pictures should be discernible from that distance, as well. Otherwise, there's no one right answer as to what our banner should have, though I have seen certain combinations work well:

- Featured book cover image, author name, and author portrait
- Giant book cover image and a quote from the book, from the back summary, or from a positive review
- Book cover images from a single series in order together with text identifying the genre of that series
- Large author image, large author name, with several book cover images

When I'm doing an author-appearance signing event, like a comic book convention, I'll use several banners together to communicate that I have published multiple series. It's a lot more likely that one of the three series will catch a passerby's eye and draw their view down to see me and the table. In order to facilitate this, I usually have my six-foot banners set up about eight feet in the air, therefore with the bottom of the banner ending just after the table line.

If I'm lucky, then they will realize that I have books to offer and will approach my booth to learn more about my books from me and examine my books more closely. Here's an example of two of my banners:

As I moved on to multiple series, I increased my booth size and started having three banners at the back. This allowed me to show three distinct and different sides of me. I made sure the banners all had the same style so that there was visual harmony between them.

DISPLAY ESSENTIAL TWO: HORIZONTAL BANNERS

The front of our table is a curious space. We don't want it to compete with what's on our table or draw the eye away, and we don't want to compete with our vertical banners and create confusion.

For the longest time, I left the front of my table covered with a black tablecloth and nothing more. After watching people at events for a long time, I noticed something. Vertical banners serve to bring their eyes down to the table. Alternately, a horizontal banner along the front of our table can help draw tired eyes up to our display. Horizontal banners could serve as a way of telling them, "Hey, I know you're tired, but there's something cool here."

READERS WANTED

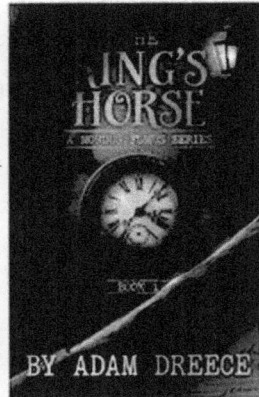

ADAMDREECE.COM

The trick is, of course, to have banners that don't overwhelm our display and to have a tabletop that is the star of the show. I experimented, learning along the way that the simpler and cleaner I kept the horizontal banner, the better it worked. Ultimately, I came up with this design which allowed me to communicate clearly in what genres I wrote and what I was after.

People who saw that horizontal banner clearly understood that I wrote books and what genres I had to offer them. At very busy and visually overwhelming events, this banner allowed people to immediately know I wrote and sold books. If they loved books, then they should come over because they were wanted at my booth. The banners reinforced my brand and articulated who I was looking to connect with.

Whatever we decide to do, our banner setup needs to work for us instead of against us. More importantly, it has to make good, clear sense to those we're trying to attract. I discourage having a busy front banner, busy vertical banners on the sides, and a busy table cloth or table runner. Our books should be the star of the show on our center stage: the well-organized tabletop.

DISPLAY ESSENTIAL THREE: THE WELL-ORGANIZED TABLETOP

The tabletop is where it all happens. Potential readers' attentions have been drawn up or down, and it's time for them to be thrilled by the main showcase.

One of the biggest mistakes I've seen, if not the biggest, is authors making stacks of their books in piles with the covers face the ceiling. Sometimes it looks more like they've built a book wall to keep passersby from seeing them. Why is this a no-no? Firstly, because our book cover is an asset to draw people in closer. The books should be angled so that people can see them. Whenever I see books displayed like that, I think of swap meets and flea markets, where books are piled to be sold with no sense of value for what they really are. Another reason to not do this is we aren't there to hide, so however we set things up, we need to be visible and present.

What should we do?

Just like a theater company would invest in stage sets, we invest in display stands—like the acrylic tabletop easel stands available from retail office supply stores. Tabletop easels allow books to be displayed at an angle with the cover facing out. Tiered display and deep display holders add interest and show off book covers. Also, a strong rectangular crate or shelf can be used to create a raised stage for the books and series we want to feature prominently on our tabletop display.

The deep-display ones on the ends can be used to display multiple copies of smaller books, while the tiered one located in the middle at the top provides four book slots to cohesively show a series. The angled easel display in the middle directly on the tabletop is great for larger books and hardcovers. Here's the same tabletop setup populated with my books.

When the books are leaned back on the easel displays, they can be seen from a distance as well as close up.

For variety, I like to place a copy of a book turned over to show the back-of-the-book cover blurb in front of the same book on a stand.

Potential readers can read the back-of-the-book blurb without touching it. That works great for those with drinks in hand as well as those who don't want to pick up my book out of a sense of obligation to purchase it before they're ready.

There are also some stores, like Brodart.com, that sell wooden stands which are outstanding. I have one that comes apart for easy transport and is great for holding a series as well as creating height.

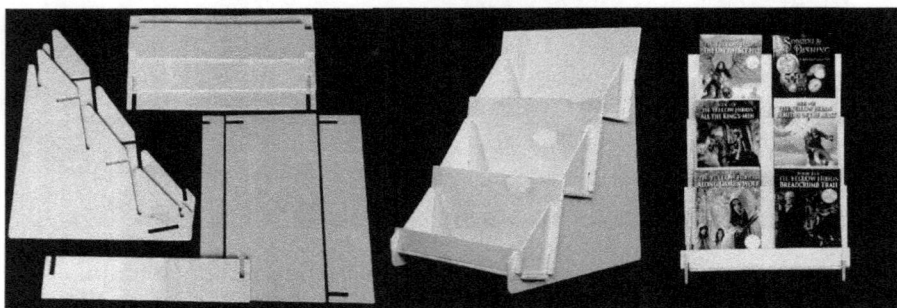

Our table should neither seem too busy nor too sparse, though I would choose sparse over busy because it's easier for a passerby to make sense of a straightforward display. If we've got many different books (I have eleven titles in print as of the first edition of this book), we can run out of space easily. We need room for our books, for our bookmarks, and a bit of empty visual space to show them all off.

On a five-foot long table (short by most signing standards), that can be a challenge. With practice and forethought, a small table can be made into a well-organized tabletop. Usually we set the focus on the latest books or series, with the rest supporting it. Often, this is what I use my elevated platform to highlight.

These elements together create a display that is engaging, interesting to look at, and easier to visually digest for someone throwing a glance my way.

Last but not least, when we have our table or booth first set up, we double check our entire display from the point of view of people who will be coming toward us. Can potential readers see our vertical banners the way we have them set up? Will most people come from a direction other than we assumed? Are our horizontal banners even and our tabletop displays organized and visually interesting?

Taking a few minutes to consider these things can be tremendously valuable. On more than one occasion, I've been in such a rush that only when I stopped to look at it like a potential reader did I recognize I'd done it all wrong. Rather than deciding it was good enough, I grabbed a cup of tea and then made the needed changes. Did it transform an okay day into a fantastic day? I have no idea, but I do know that if I hadn't made the changes, it would have haunted me all day. That would have affected my mindset, and ultimately how I engaged with passersby.

A TALE OF A LONE BOOK

Years ago I was at a convention where my booth neighbor was a first-time author in his late sixties. He had a science fiction book with a plot that centered around asteroid mining. He had his book on an easel display, and its simple cover caught some interest but didn't seem to inspire passersby.

Nevertheless, potential readers still stopped at his table and chatted with him about his book. For some reason that he couldn't understand, a lot of potential readers interested in his book didn't pick it up. More importantly, they didn't buy his book. The problem was that in the middle of his barren table, he had put one book on an easel stand.

One book.

As the first of the two days reached its final hours, we had a conversation that opened the door for me to offer some help to my fellow author. To cut a long story short, I had him give me some more books; then I made swirls on the edge of the tabletop using those books. I hypothesized that people assumed his lonely book was his only copy. Now people would see aesthetic abundance.

The net result? He sold more books in those last two hours than he had all day. The final hours of the second day turned a failed convention book signing into a success for him.

DRESSING THE PART

Another element of the overall display is us. At my first book signing event at that comic convention, I dressed in jeans and had a t-shirt with my book cover printed on it. Over the course of the weekend, I realized I was missing a huge opportunity to really connect with potential readers of my book's genre.

The next time I attended an event, I wore a steampunk vest, monocle, and a Victorian period shirt. became part of the presentation, and people started to come over to ask me where I got my clothing or just to take a picture with me.

As I started writing other genres, I started to vary my Author Persona's costuming a bit more. If I was focusing on my science fiction novel, The Man of Cloud 9, it didn't make sense to use steampunk costuming. Instead, I chose more of a Steve Jobs look.

My point isn't that we need to dress up, but rather we have an opportunity to costume our Author Persona to add an extra element to that presentation. When I go to schools to give a talk, I usually dress up for fun and to be memorable. If I'm attending a writers' conference, I dress in modern business casual. Why? Because every opportunity is different, and I'm not seeking to draw extra attention at writers' conferences.

SUMMING IT UP

To paraphrase from one of my favorite movies, Megamind: The difference between a villain and a super-villain is presentation. In our case, the difference between an author and an author who gets attention is presentation. When we're thinking things through from the approaching readers' perspective, then we're in the right mindset to deliver a memorable presentation of our books and ourselves.

How we set up our signing space matters. I've had signings where all I was given was a two-foot-by-two-foot folding card table. While that was a ruthless challenge deciding what I would present and what I wouldn't, I wasn't fazed. All the same principles of excellent presentation apply no matter how small or grand my book signing table.

A good friend of mine, author Suzy Vadori, uses a fountain sculpture full of lollipops as part of her display. Why? Because her first book in The Fountain Series is called The Fountain, and her tabletop fountain looks almost precisely like the one on the cover of her first book. It adds an extra three-dimensional element from banner and book to the actual display fountain. Lastly, it provides an engaging way to display giveaways, the lollipops as well as giving her a gimmick to offer people to make a wish, which also ties to the book. It's a great example of pulling a lot of different elements together and making it work beautifully.

On the other side, I've seen some rookie mistakes from authors that with a bit of preparation, we personally can avoid. First, we bring our own black tablecloths and draping to every signing event. It doesn't matter if they guarantee they will have precisely what we need or request. We bring our own. Always.

At one signing, I arrived and discovered the black tablecloth I was promised was actually bright red plastic. That would have not worked at all for my colorful books, so bringing my own black tablecloth saved me from unnecessary stress. While some authors decide to use whatever's provided, that's a real risk. If nothing is offered but a table, that's worse than an inappropriate table covering. A battered and stained wooden table—or worse, a dull, grey plastic folding one! —takes away from even a top-notch tabletop presentation. Imagine that harsh contrast with our professional banners enticing people to our slapdash signing space revealing all of our boxes and other stuff that should be hidden out of view under the table.

We don't have need anything fancy. We don't even need acrylic stands. We can stack books and lean one against the pile, so that our cover is easy to view for people walking by. All we need is to be thoughtful and intentional, to take seriously how we present ourselves and our books to our potential readers, and it will make a world of difference.

−11−

THREE STORIES

When we put ourselves out there as authors, we will have memorable encounters. Some will challenge us; some will encourage us; some will affect us. Every story will change us because each one becomes a part of us.

THE ONE-STAR REVIEW AT POINT BLANK RANGE

No author fantasizes doing about a book signing event where someone shows up to their table and decides to unload on them with sharp and loud criticisms of their books. The fear of an unreasonable anti-fan confronting us can keep many of us from even considering author appearances. That said, even when we know the types of people we meet at signing events (Critical Thing #3), people will surprise us—which is very much what this first story demonstrates.

I had an anti-fan, an Angry Jerk personality type, who trolled me online mercilessly. Relentless, he went on and on about how terrible my first book, *Along Came a Wolf*, was. I feared that someone like that anti-fan could show up in person, but event after event passed without that kind of aggressive harassment. Then one day, I learned how well-developed my Author Persona really was.

My wife and I had reserved a booth at a very large comic book convention that I attend yearly. Sales had been strong from the start, and I was just returning from giving a well-received writers' talk to a packed room. Several of the attendees of my presentation had followed me back to my booth. After we all discussed writing for a few minutes, most left. One guy with a very intense gaze remained standing a few feet back from the table.

An anti-fan was staring directly at me.

He couldn't have been more than twenty years old. His dark hair was a little long and tangled. He was flexing his fingers, and I couldn't tell if it was from anxiety or anger. Once the other people had left, my online anti-fan looked me dead in the eyes and said. "I liked your talk, but I hate your books."

Upon hearing those words, I froze. While my heart skipped a beat, I didn't flinch.

Taking a worn copy of my second book out from his coat with a trembling hand, he shook it at me. "This is terrible. You're a terrible writer. The plot and story and characters are terrible."

Taking a breath, I realized that the moment I'd feared was really here. Oddly, it didn't feel how I had thought it would. Instead of feeling rattled, I felt more ready for battle. I assumed a solid stance with my feet rooted to the ground. Everyone's entitled to their own opinion, and I knew better than to allow a situation to become a scene. There's nothing like having a video of us yelling at someone posted on YouTube to damage our author brand.

Counting to five in my head first, I then replied, "Well, I'm sorry you feel that way."

The guy came right up to the booth table's edge. "No, you need to understand that you are terrible! These Yellow Hoods books are just garbage!"

I could sense my wife was ready to jump to my defense, though she knew it wasn't necessary. She might only be 5'2", while I'm 6'2", but she's a mama bear crossed with a wolverine when it comes to defending me (never mind our children). In the early days of our relationship, the petite blonde love of my life slipped in between me and a 6'6" man who was threatening me. Undaunted, she started stabbing him with her index finger while yelling even more loudly at him than he was yelling at me.

I gave a light touch on her arm, telling her everything was okay, and I stepped toward the anti-fan. Seeing potential readers approaching our booth, she turned to focus on them.

I took a deep breath and made sure not to cross my arms. For a few seconds, I wondered how to handle the situation. Everyone's allowed to have an opinion, but it doesn't mean we have to listen to Angry Jerks. I could have used the Critical Thing #3 tactics to deal with Jealous Hostiles and Booth Barnacles, but there was something about this young man that I felt was important to figure out. I replied with a smile. "Oh?"

He told me that he'd attended a talk the year before and had then come to the booth and bought the first two books in my steampunk-meets-fairy-tale series, *The Yellow Hoods*. He'd enjoyed both talks he'd attended but felt that the books I'd written were nothing like the talks I'd given. Both presentations had been about writing and not about my actual books.) He then shook his copy of *Breadcrumb Trail* at me again and said, "I read the first book and am halfway through the second, and this is terrible."

I took in what he said and seriously considered both his words and that he and I were still standing in front of my author booth. My lack of immediate reaction bothered him: The corner of his mouth was twitching. I got the sense that he might be the type of person who people tended to ignore.

My wife gave me a wide-eyed look, silently telling me that I needed to get rid of him. Instead, I stepped away from my book signing booth and waved for my anti-fan to join me about ten feet away. I wasn't being a glutton for punishment, nor was I wanting to tear a strip off the guy. I thought of my Author Persona core creed and mantra: Be the mentor I wish I'd had. Maybe, if I actively listened and steered this right, both he and I could come out of this experience better for it.

I chose to risk it. "So you've read all of the first book?"

"Yes," he replied with a vigorous nod. "Hated it."

"And you then went on to read the second book?"

"Yes, and I'm half-way through it." He pointed at his bookmark.

I scratched my chin and looked him over again. Something wasn't adding up. I don't know anyone who could both hate a series yet keep reading it—unless it was so bad it was good, and that was definitely not the signal my anti-fan was broadcasting.

"Do you remember the demographic that I said this series was for?" I asked, curious.

"Kids and teens and older people."

"Right. So, that said, you are aware that this wasn't written for you per se."

"I don't see how an adult could like this."

Without thinking, I said, "The series gets darker as it goes. You probably have seen that so far in book two."

"Your answer is that I have to buy more books?" He glared at me, as if he had me right where he wanted me. "No."

I stopped and thought. Then I talked about how I had evolved as a writer as I've gone, and how I had written different types of books, like *The Man of Cloud 9* and *The Wizard Killer* series. Finally, I pointed out that different books reached different types of people.

"So I have to buy different books of yours?"

Scratching the back of my head, I was determined not to give up. My hopeful side was certain that I was close to defusing his anger, though my wiser side was telling me that I was playing a far riskier game than I should. There would be no harm in just wishing him well and refusing to engage an anti-fan further, but for some reason, I felt for the guy. "No, that's not what I'm saying."

Part of me was tempted offer him a refund. Maybe that would let him walk away happier, I reasoned. No sooner had that thought come along, than I realized that would be a terrible precedent to set.

A thought dawned on me: He had come to two of my talks and had said he had enjoyed both. "Are you a writer?"

"Yes." He was about to continue, but I raised a hand, cutting him off.

My wife gave me a soul-scorching glare as she stood at the table with a reader who wanted their book signed. I flashed two fingers, signaling to her I would return momentarily, as I hoped the conversation was drawing to a conclusion.

"Do you feel that you can do better than my first two books?" I asked, without a tone of challenge or malice in my voice.

After a moment of hesitation, he answered. "Yes."

"Then please, do so. Take my books as inspiration. Don't make the same mistakes that you feel I made; do better. Do you think you learned a bunch by reading my books?"

The young man shoulders relaxed, and his gaze swept about thoughtfully. "I suppose I have."

"I did too. They aren't perfect, but you know what they were?"

He frowned at me.

"You were in my session earlier. What are the two biggest fears that authors have?" I asked.

"Finishing and judgment."

"And those books were finished, and I put them out for judgment. I know that not everyone is going to like them, even if they are of the right age or even like that type of book nine times out of ten. Someone will always love it, and someone will always hate it. But if you can get something from a book, discover something about yourself, or take inspiration from it, then it was worth your time—wouldn't you say?"

His brow furrowed as he took in what I said. He then nodded slowly.

"Thanks for sharing your opinion with me. I hope that you continue to like my talks, and hopefully, at some point, you find you really like a series of mine." I stuck out my hand.

The young man smiled and shook my hand. "Thanks for listening and . . . and being so mature about this."

He walked away, his agitation gone, and I hurried over to the reader waiting on me to sign their book.

There were several great lessons I took away that day. First, I didn't have to fear this type of situation ever again. It hadn't been as bad as I assumed, and more importantly, my confidence hadn't evaporated. Second, the time I took to build up my confidence engaging the public, to create my Author Persona, and to reinforce my author brand had paid off in ways I hadn't expected.

THE KID AND THE MOM

As authors, we aren't just writers. We are mentors and muses to other writers, yet often we have no clue about the valuable impact we have on others. Encountering writers we've motivated is always a pleasure; encountering writers we've motivated to overcome their fear and write from the heart can revitalize us—as this next story affirms.

I'm a regular speaker at young writers' conferences, and I love it. The energy and passion of the kids, the secret hope that I'm inspiring them in a way I would have loved to be inspired—it's great.

I was at a local mall doing a book signing at a bookstore. A boy, no more than twelve, with black, tight curly hair, came over to me. His eyes were wide, and he had a big grin. His mom trailed after him.

"I know you," he said, pointing at me.

"You do?" I replied, raising an eyebrow comically and putting on the exaggerated suspicious expression that I used to make my own kids laugh. "Where from?"

"I was in a class of yours at the young writers' conference."

"He was, indeed," said Mom, putting her hands on his shoulders as a big smile appeared on her face.

"Well, I hope you liked it." I smiled, always loving to run into the future J.K. Rowlings and Neil Gaimans.

The boy raised his chin proudly. "You helped me stop being scared, and I wrote a book for my mom. I've wanted to do it for a long time."

I looked over at Mom, and she had tears in her eyes. "It was great," she said, hugging him. "Thank you so much."

"My absolute pleasure," I replied.

As they walked away, several people approached, asking questions about the boy and my books. It was a great day.

Since then, I carry with me everywhere that no matter how sales are going, how lost I might feel writing my latest manuscript, or how down on myself I am, just being out there in public helps inspire others.

And they in turn inspire me back.

This is one of my happy thoughts I keep tucked away for getting me out of bad moods, as per Critical Thing #2.

GREEN JACKET MAN

As authors, our work can do more than simply inspire someone; it can hold a much deeper meaning for them. There are many ways to reach people, particularly those who might not be the go-to-a-bookstore types, as this final story reveals.

I was doing a signing at Indigo, a local big-box bookstore. As I was talking with a family, I noticed a man in the background. He was glancing over his shoulder at me every now and then. After the family left, he hesitantly stepped into view.

He appeared in his mid-twenties. He was hunched over, with the collar of his beaten-up, green, military jacket pulled up high. His hair was short and uneven, and he had a stringy beard. Judging by his size, he looked like he'd normally be a physically intimidating figure. However, for some reason, he read like a wounded wolf.

Looking in my direction long enough for me to notice him, the man in the threadbare field jacket quickly broke eye contact and waved a finger at my *Yellow Hoods* books.

"I like your books." Once again, he made eye contact and broke it off.

There was something in the way he said those four words that gave me pause.

I've learned over the years that we never entirely know our typical reader and that we need to dismantle the snap judgments, unconscious bias, and assumptions our upbringing and experiences may have given us. In the same way we don't want our books judged by their covers, we can't know what's on the inside of people.

Nevertheless, I had a hard time imagining this guy reading my *Yellow Hoods* books. I felt compelled to ask the obvious question. "Have you read them?"

Taking a moment and turning to face me, he nodded and offered a fleeting look. "Yeah. The first two. I read them many times. I really liked them," he said, straightening up a bit as emotion rang clearly in his words.

"Do you mind if I ask where?"

He nodded. "At the Cancer Center."

My eyes went wide as I remembered that a year and a half before, I'd donated two dozen books of mine to the local hospital. "Oh, wow."

"They got me through chemo. They're really good. I wish I had money to buy them, but I don't."

Staring at the ground, my eyes watered. Blinking repeatedly, I thought of the friends of mine who had gone through chemotherapy. They'd spoken about how brutal it had been, both physically and mentally. I drew in a settling breath. This time, it was me fighting to give him eye contact.

"Please, never stop writing. Those books mean a lot to me," he said, pulling his green jacket tightly around him.

It took me a minute to collect my thoughts and get my emotions back in check. When I finally looked up, planning to give him signed copies for free, he was gone.

The weight of his words are still fresh in my mind. They remind me of how powerful stories can be and how we never really know who will fall in love with our books.

I've met men like muscly brick walls, with what seemed like permanent scowls, who became excited over my steampunk-meets-fairy-tale stories. I've even met doting grandmothers who said, "Nana loves her good post-apocalyptic action! Adam, give me some of your Wizard Killer books."

Whenever I start losing steam with my writing, I remember his request of me. In that moment, he made me a better person and a better author. Even thinking about this story makes me emotional and reminds me that being an author is about more than writing and publishing stories then showing up to book signing events.

Why I Shared These Stories

By scheduling and showing up to book signings and author appearance events, we do a lot more than promote our books and build our brand. We create brand-new stories with our fans.

Imagine it from their perspective. They were in their own little world when a stranger asked, "May I tell you about my books?" They turned and discovered a smiling, friendly face with an amazing display of books that seemed to have just materialized beside them. The stranger goes on to talk about the incredible tales waiting on the pages of the books, as well as some personal adventures as a writer. The reader, giddy at meeting someone so interesting who writes books they want to read, decides to take a picture to show friends and post on social media. The stranger seems genuinely surprised but agrees. Grateful, the reader quickly hugs the author then walks from the table with both social currency and signed books in a bag, anticipating that first chance to start reading.

Suddenly, the reader tears off after their friends. They call out to them, hoping to share the story and show off the signed books and the photograph with a new favorite author.

For authors, our own experience is at least equally moving. There we are at our booths or tables, tired and frustrated. It doesn't help that the foot traffic for the past hour has been sparse to nonexistent.

We give ourselves a mental kick out of our doldrums just before a person moves out of voice range. We offer a half-hearted and far too quiet, "May I tell you about my books?"

To our surprise, the person stops and turns. To our astonishment, their face lights up as they appreciate our banners and admire our book display. Then they finally focus on us. We can't help but smile from ear to ear with eager excitement that maybe, just maybe, this potential reader is a fan in the making.

As the person steps forward, our pulse accelerates and our exhaustion evaporates. Before we know it, our arms are moving about wildly as we offer an impassioned description of our stories. Our conversation spills over into the subject of writing, itself, and we receive compliments for our perseverance and drive. We realize it's time to accept that we have indeed earned our title as author. With a bag of books in hand, our wonderful, new fan asks if we would allow a selfie with them.

Selfie? What are we, a celebrity? And in actual fact, we are; a mini-celebrity, yes, but we are one nonetheless.

With a surprise hug, the fan's fan walks away then starts to run off, chasing after friends. Their bag of books is held high, and their excited voice is riding above the dull roar of the room: "Guys, I just met the coolest author ever!"

In a blink, it's over, and they've disappeared. That moment, that joy, is a top candidate for a happy thought we'll use to turn a sour mood sweet again.

I've shared my stories to remind us that while fan emails are wonderful and can be charged with emotion, and chatting with people on Twitter, Facebook, Discord, or other social media platforms is great, there's nothing like the in-person stories from book signings and author appearances to leave a lasting impression on our souls.

Recently, a father came up to me and told me how his teenage son had never read a chapter book until a friend brought him to a book launch of mine. Since then, his son has read all of my books and has moved on to other local authors. That father finds me at every local convention, shakes my hand, and thanks me again for making his son excited to read.

Putting ourselves out there may very well get us a One-Star Reviewer moment or two, but it will bring us Little Boy and His Mom and the Green Jacket Man stories, and that more than makes up for it.

–12–

BRINGING IT ALL TOGETHER

Some people sell their books like they are selling a bobble-head toy that's available everywhere. There's no sense of just how wondrous and amazing, never mind unique, their books are. In this day and age, "meeting the author" is social currency, shared all across the social media spectrum.

Simply standing at a fantastic booth, with well-laid-out books and promotional gifts, isn't enough. We are the real magic. In our Author Persona armor, mentally ready to engage potential readers and make them into lifelong fans, it doesn't matter how awkward it might feel at first. We will be the reason why hundreds, if not thousands, of people will walk away feeling personally connected to our books. We will also be why we sell three hundred while the meek or the hard-selling author two tables over sells thirty.

Even with the best of preparation, our event will always be vulnerable to weather, traffic, or a sports game that vacuums up all the people. Even then, we never know when we're going to have a moment that becomes an author story—like the kid who overcame his fear to write a story for his mom or the man in the green jacket who read our books again and again during chemotherapy. There's nothing that can lift our spirits more than seeing a stranger leap into the air and shout, "Holy crap, my favorite author's here in person!" We hold on to those moments. We use them to embolden ourselves to live openly as the Author Persona we want to see in the world. And we stand ready to get more of those kinds of stories.

Remember that when I started, I had no idea what I was doing. The only thing I knew was that I didn't want to fail. I learned that it wasn't about selling a product, but about building my author brand, engaging potential readers and organically hand-selling at an event, and extending my reach as an author beyond that in-person event. I learned to build up my Author Persona from what I admired most in others and knew was also within me. I got so used to it in time that I feel more like myself with it on than off. There's no reason why any author can't do what I've done—or even do it better.

Having that first successful book signing doesn't even start with a small step, but with simply the willingness to try. From there, try out one element of one Critical Thing, and then another. We'll move forward an inch at a time, but at one point we'll look up and realize we've gone a mile. We can do this.

Let's lose our fear, embrace these steps, and get out there and delight our fans with a book signing!

Thanks for Reading

Reviews are powerful. They are more than just us sharing our important voice and opinion; they are also about telling the world that people are reading a book.

Many don't realize that without enough reviews, your favorite independently published, or indie, authors are excluded from important newsletters and other opportunities that could otherwise help them get the word out. So, if you have the opportunity to share in writing your opinion about this book, I would greatly appreciate your review.

Don't know how to write a review? Check out AdamDreece.com/WriteAReview for details like what to say and where to post it. If you are good to go, then posting your review to GoodReads.com and your favorite online retailer would be a greatly appreciated.

Don't miss out on sneak peeks and news. Join my newsletter at: AdamDreece.com/newsletter.

About the Author

Off and on for 25 years, Adam Dreece wrote short stories enjoyed by his friends and family. Regularly, his career in technology took precedence over his writing career, so he set aside his dream of one day, maybe, becoming a published author.

After a life-altering event, Adam decided to make more changes in his life, including never missing a night of reading stories to his kids again because of work, and becoming an author.

He then wrote his first book for his daughter, Along Came a Wolf. With it, he created The Yellow Hoods series. Since then, he has written and published a dozen books. Adam is a frequent public speaker at conferences and schools, giving talks to people of all ages on writing, publishing, and in-person author events.

He lives in Calgary, Alberta, Canada with his awesome wife and amazing kids.

Adam blogs about writing and what he's up to at AdamDreece.com. He is on Twitter @AdamDreece and Instagram @AdamDreece. And lastly, feel free to email him at Adam.Dreece@ADZOPublishing.com.

Acknowledgments

This book would not have been possible without the help of amazing friends, beta readers, proofreaders, and editors. Thank you to everyone who helped make this book happen. Without you, this would have continued to sit as a pile of notes scattered between various notebooks throughout my house and taking up eternal room in my head.

I'd like to call out a few folks who were very much instrumental in getting this book into your hands:

Jackson Dean Chase. Thank you, my friend and fellow indie author, for poking me for years to write this book.

Jess Alter and Mike Bybee. Thank you for your encouragement, your insightful edits, and being part of the team to make this happen.

Stacey Kondla. Thank you for your support through all the various forms this project has gone.

Joshua Pantalleresco. Apparently, unconditional friendship comes in the form of an unassuming storyteller and podcaster.

Also, thank you to: Gary, Judith, Faye, M.L., Tammy, and everyone else who helped make this book possible.

ALSO BY ADAM DREECE

The Yellow Hoods

Discover the original, best-selling, young adult series that launched Adam Dreece's career and created the world of Mondus Fumus. Join Tee, Elly, Nikolas Klaus and their friends as their lives are turned upside in the pursuit of the first steam engine.

This gripping and snarky series is great fun for kids (9+) and adults.

Available in eBook, paperback, and audiobook formats.

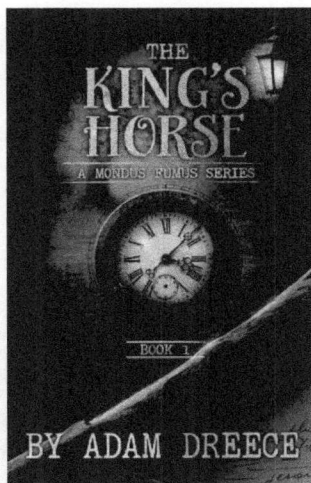

The King's Horse - Book 1

An all-new series, picking up with Christina Creangle and Mounira from The Yellow Hoods, and bringing to life Black Beauty, the Muffin Man, and more.

Available in eBook, paperback, and audiobook formats.

The Wizard Killer

In the post-apocalyptic fantasy world of Mondus Inferno, where once flying cities ruled by Wizards dotted the skies, a man with no name fights to survive long enough to learn his past. This high action, episodic series waits for no one. So buckle up and watch your back. For ages 12+. Available in eBook, paperback, and audiobook formats.

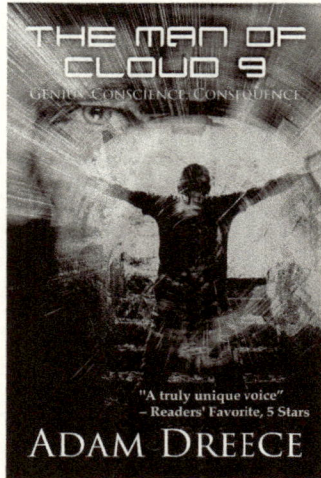

The Man of Cloud 9

    In the late 21st century, a brilliant inventor is on the verge of reshaping human history with his nanobot-cloud technology when an old enemy discovers his greatest secret. Will he be able to stop and save the lives of those closest to him, or will he risk everything and everyone for a chance to make it? This sci-fi thriller will have you stopping and looking at the world around you, realizing that this future isn't that far away. For ages 14+.

    Available in eBook and paperback formats.